THIS BOOK BELONGS TO

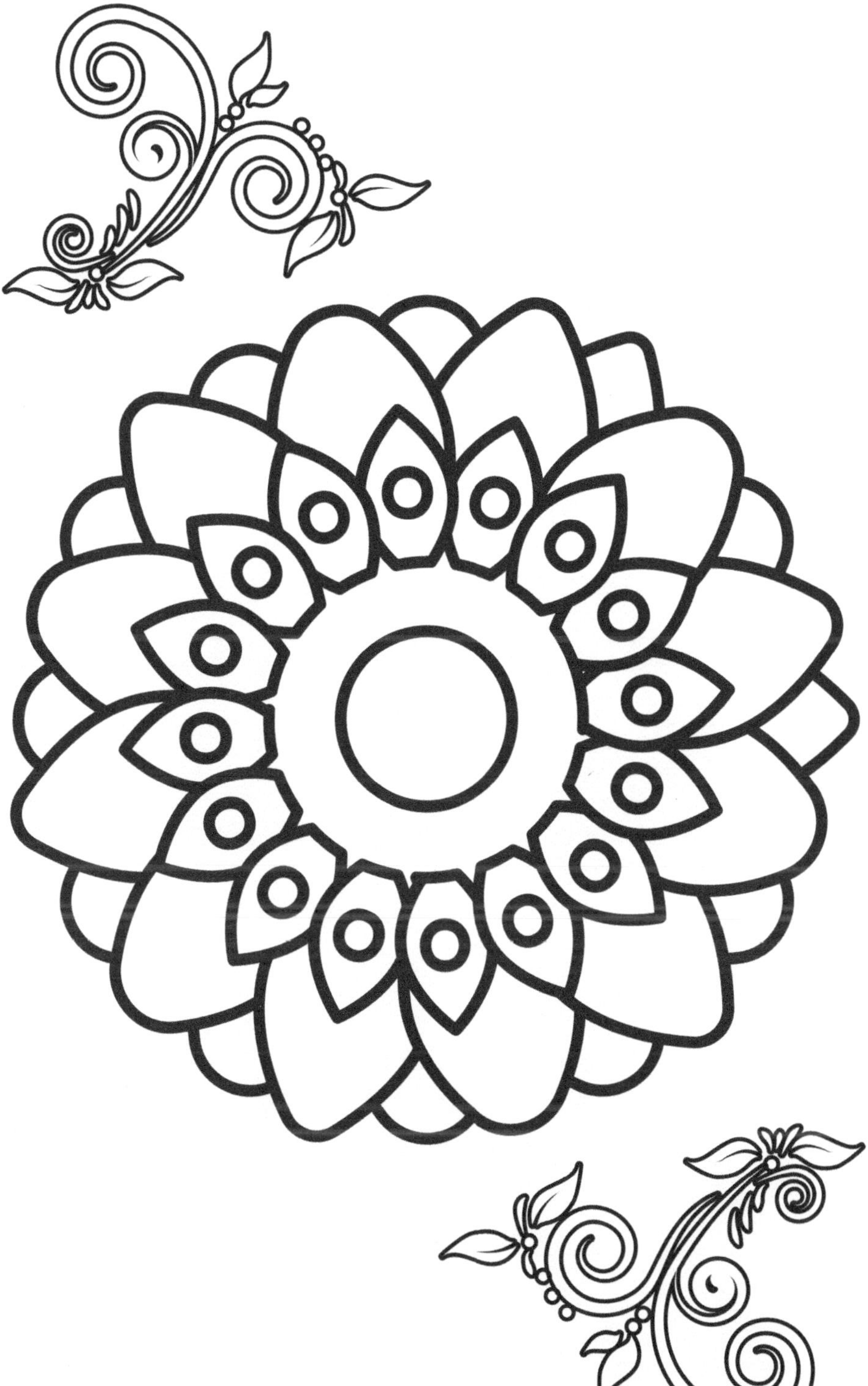

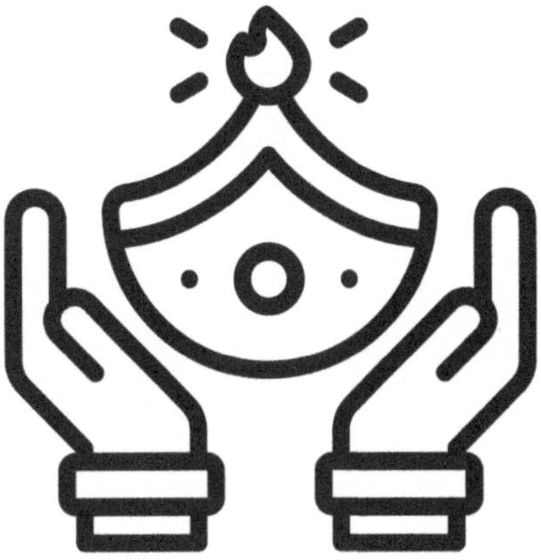

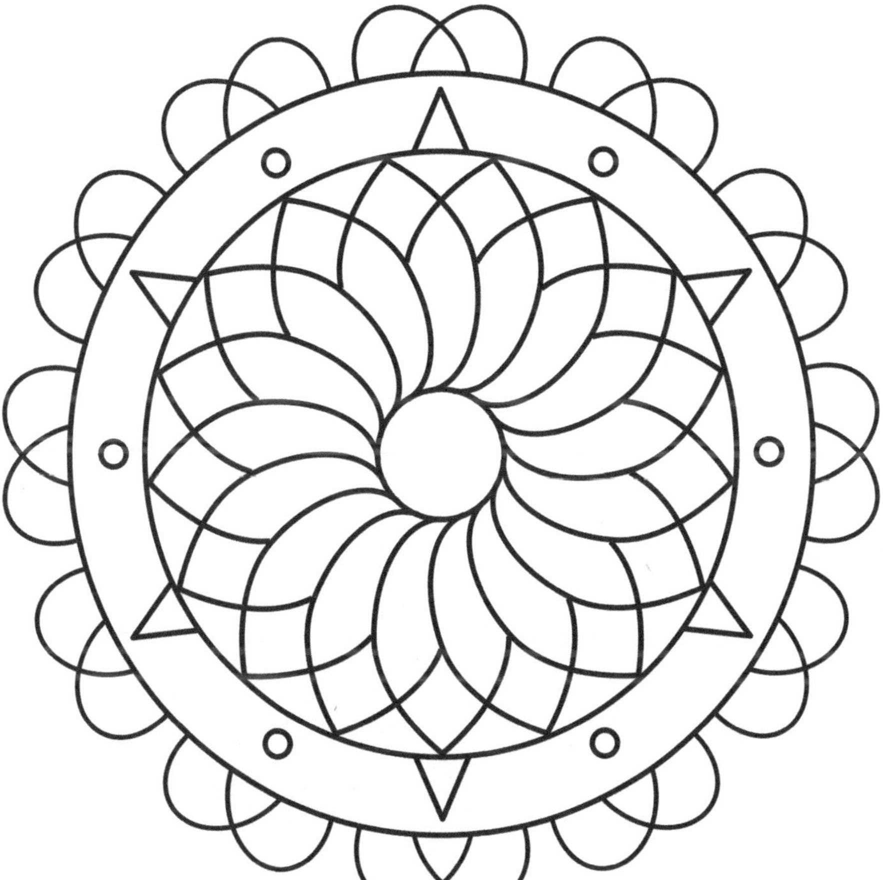

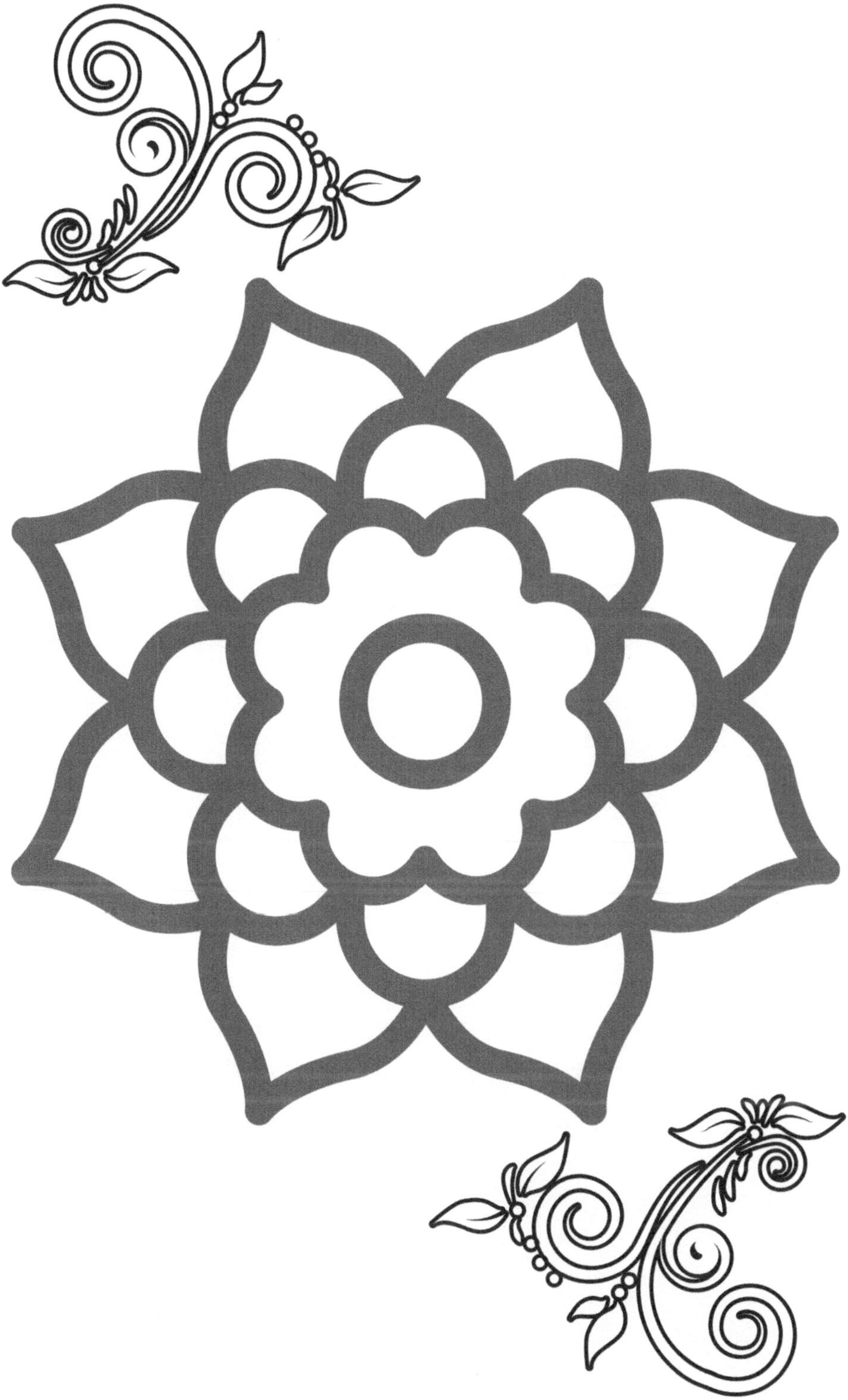

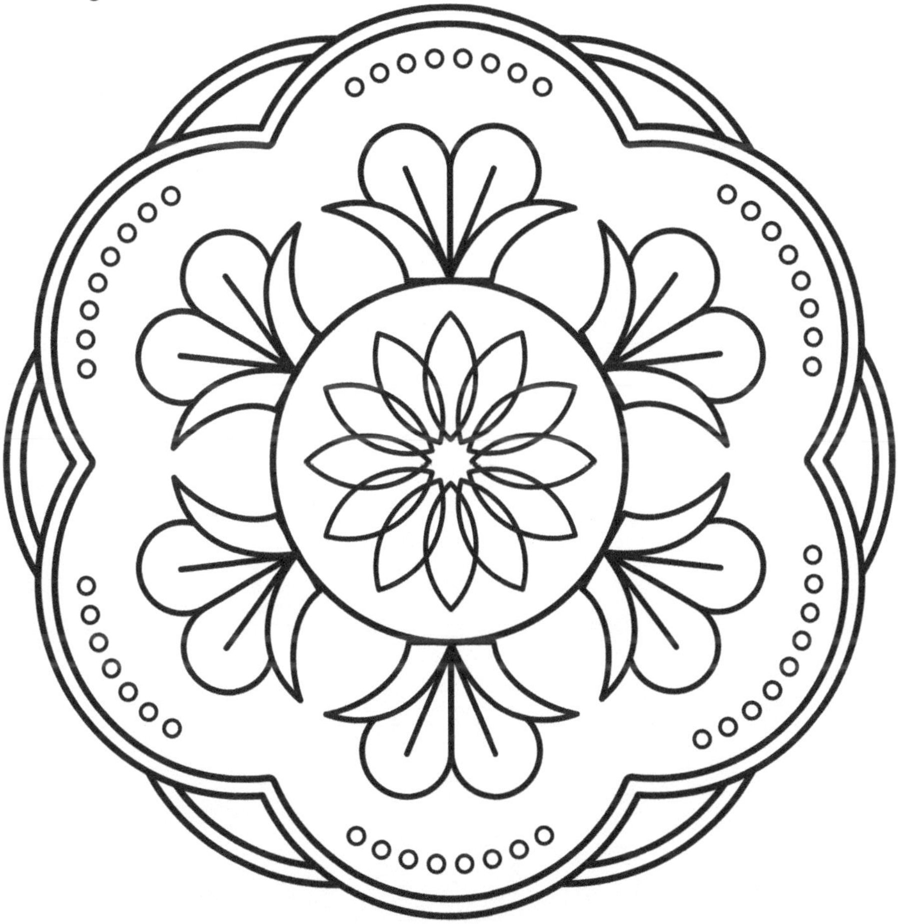

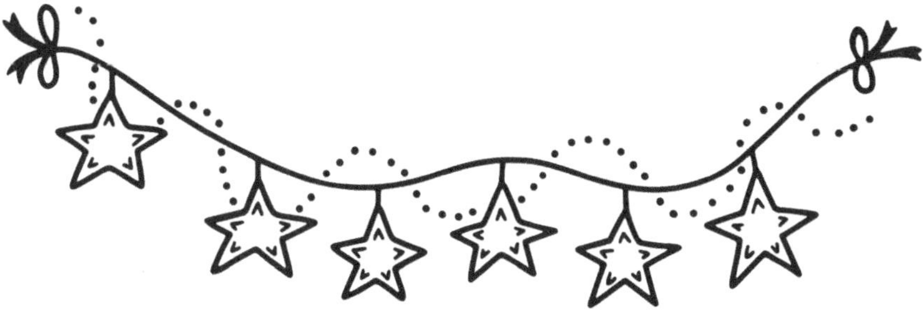

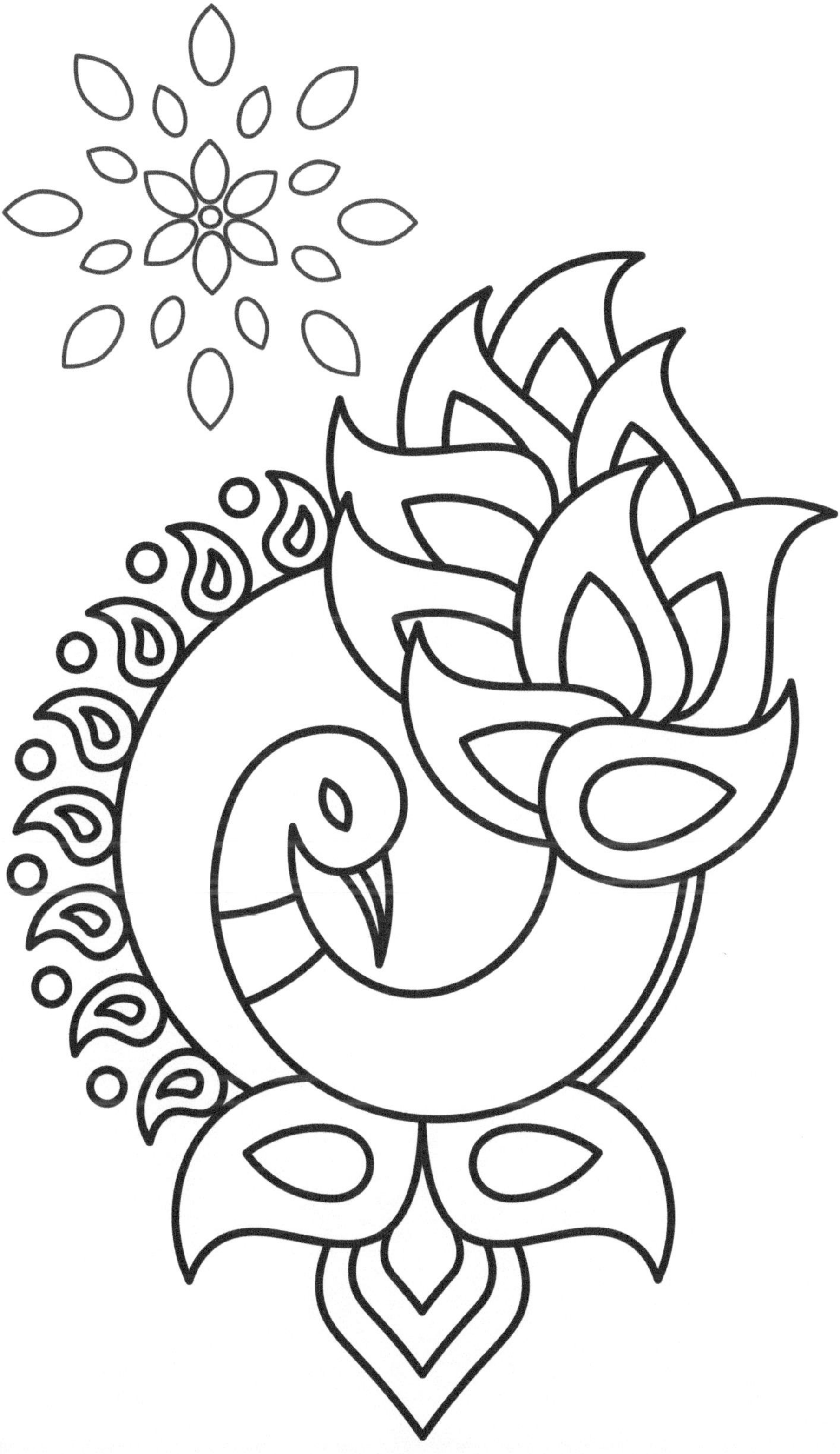

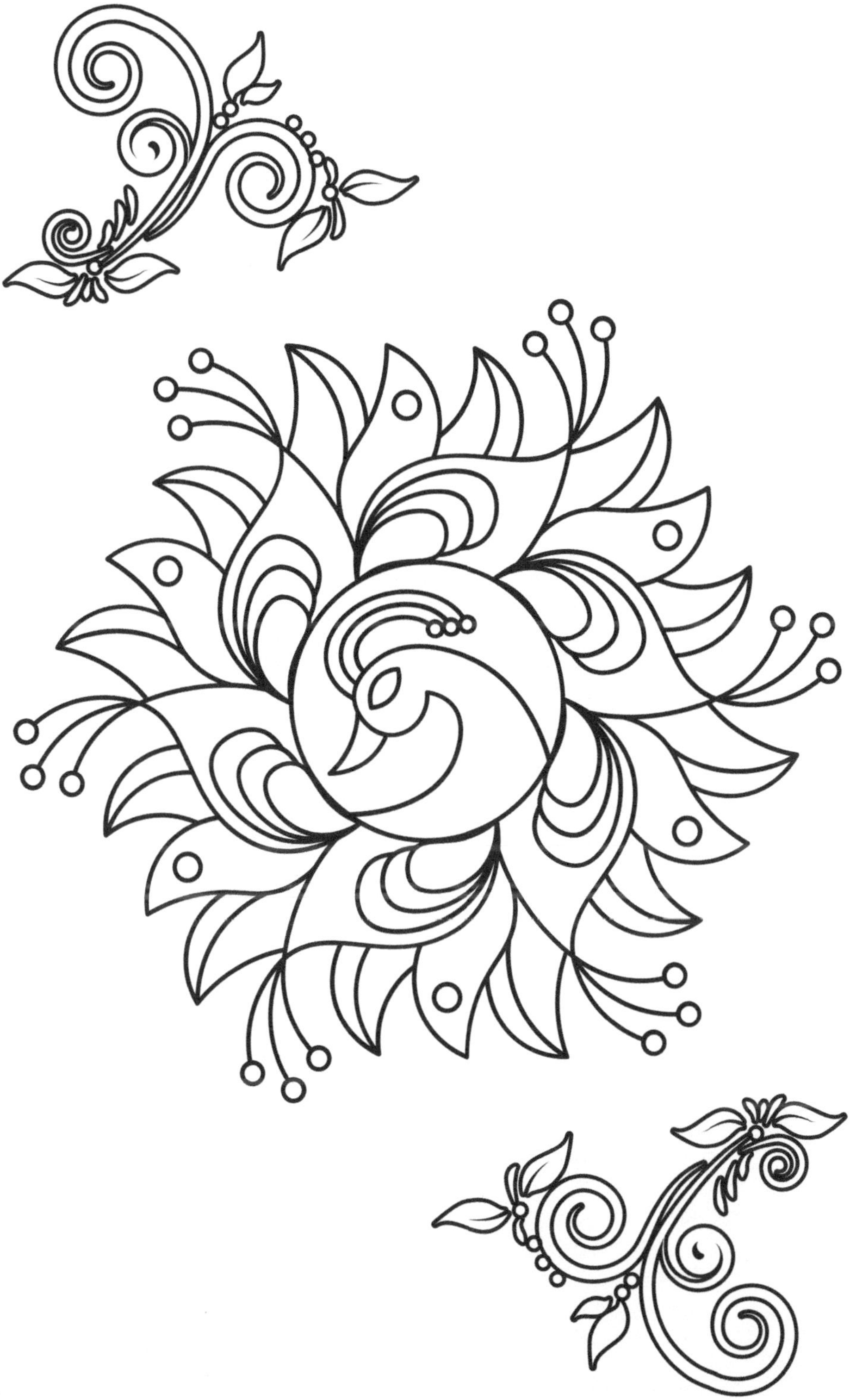

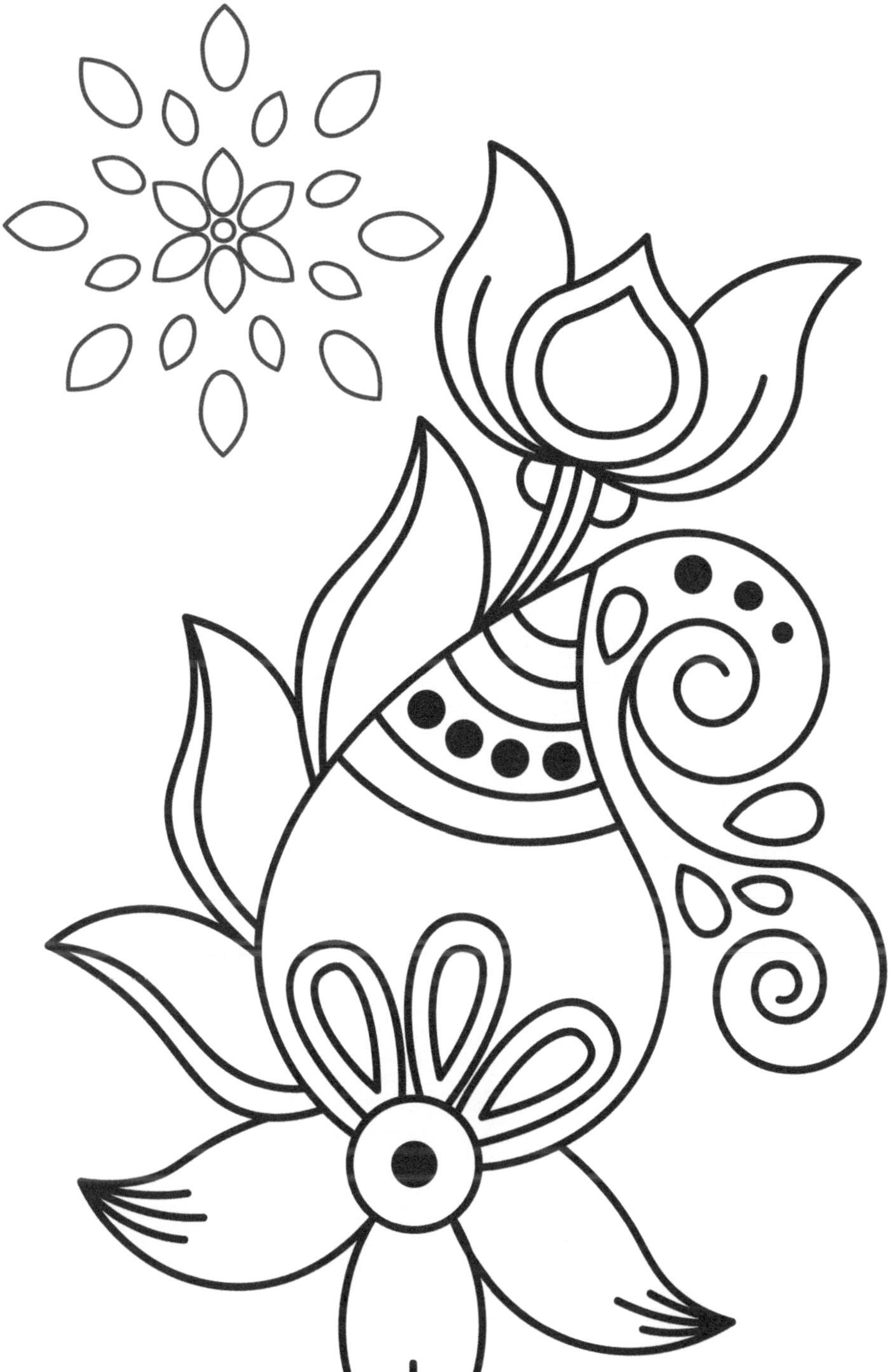

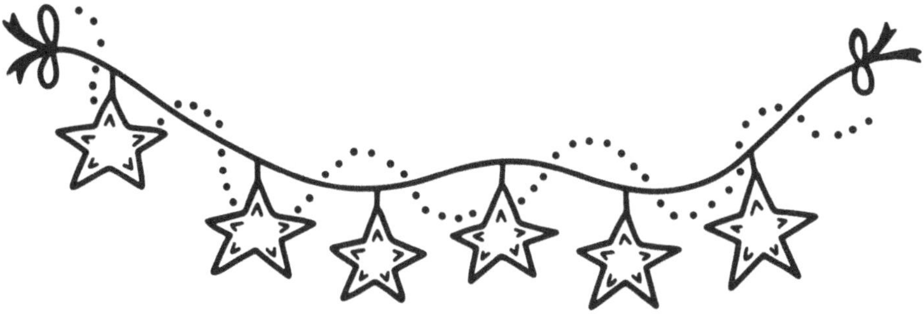

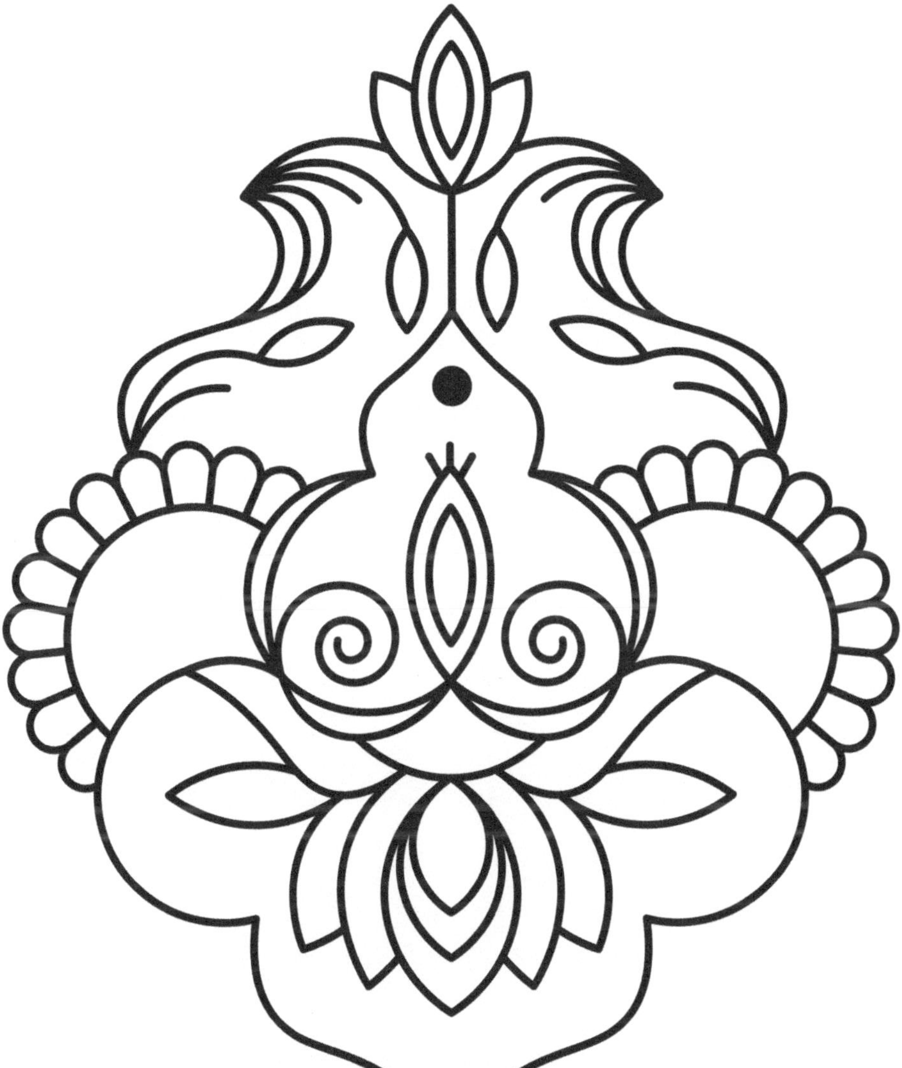

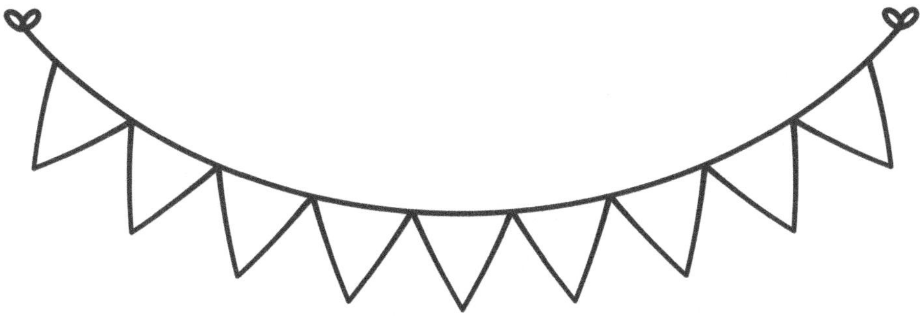

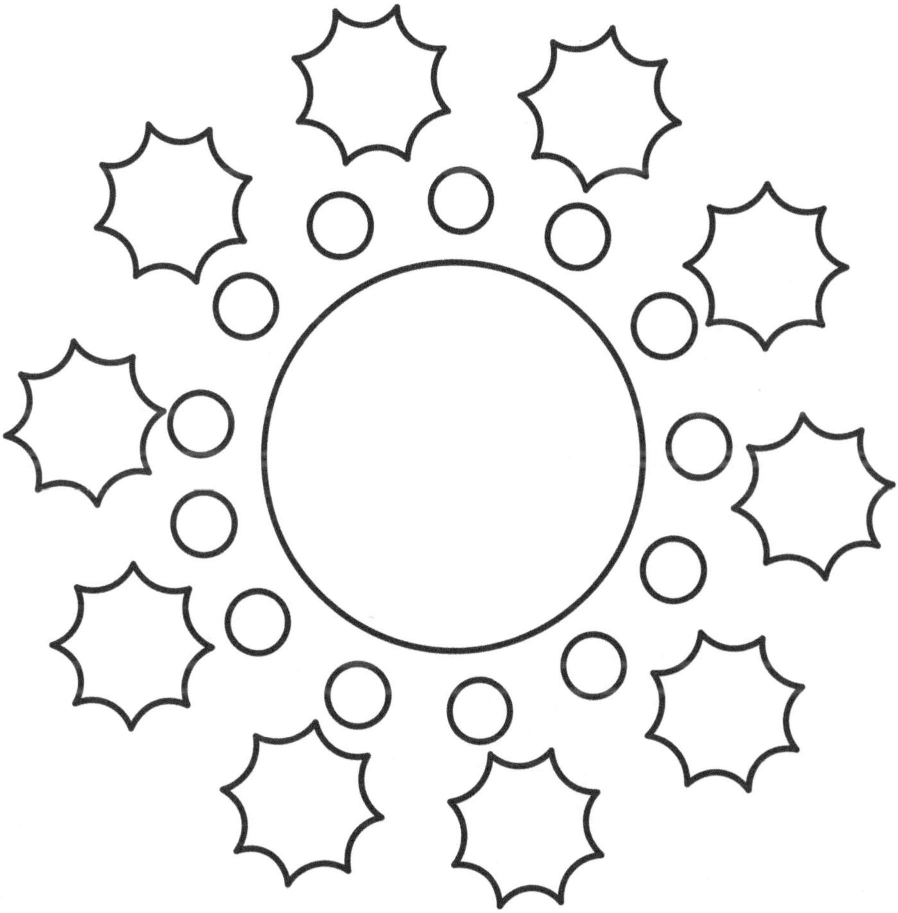

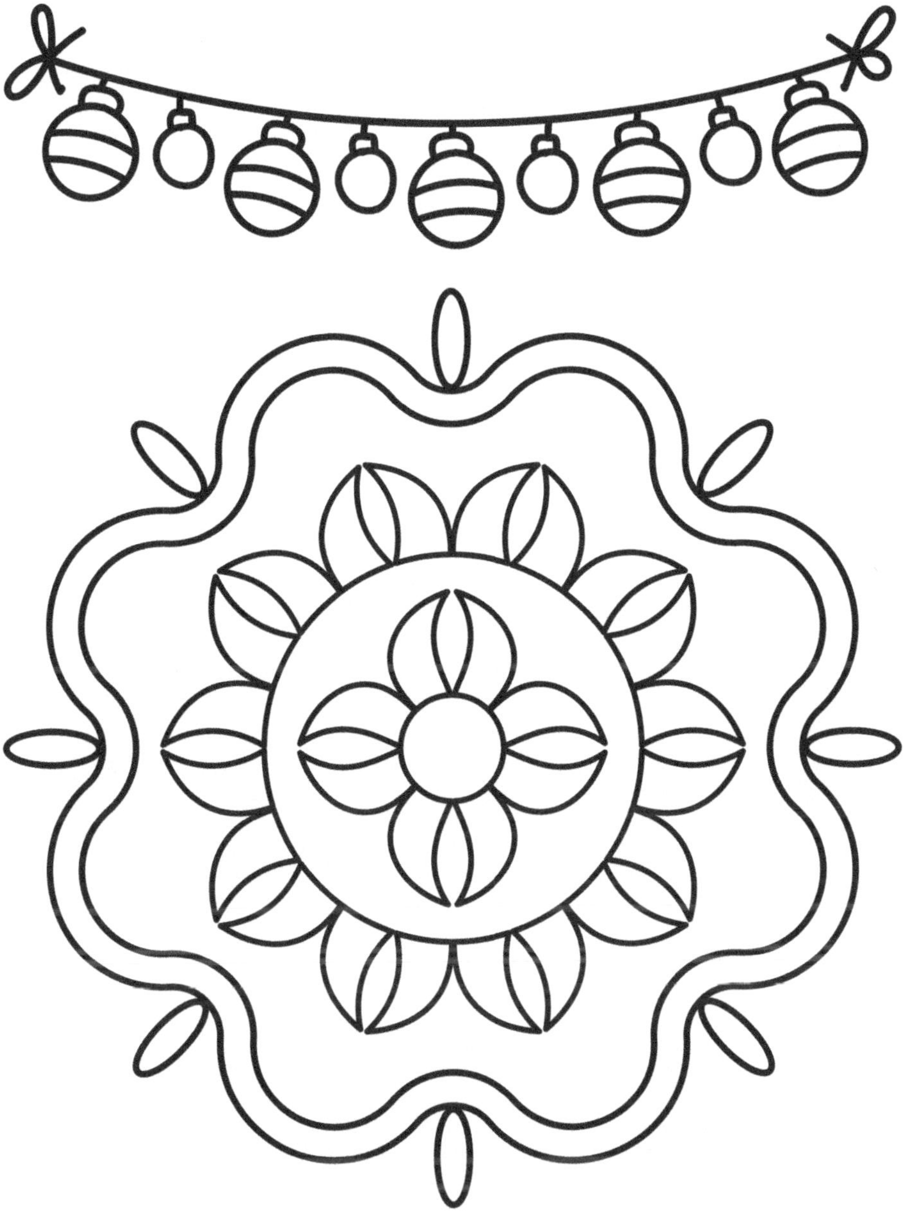

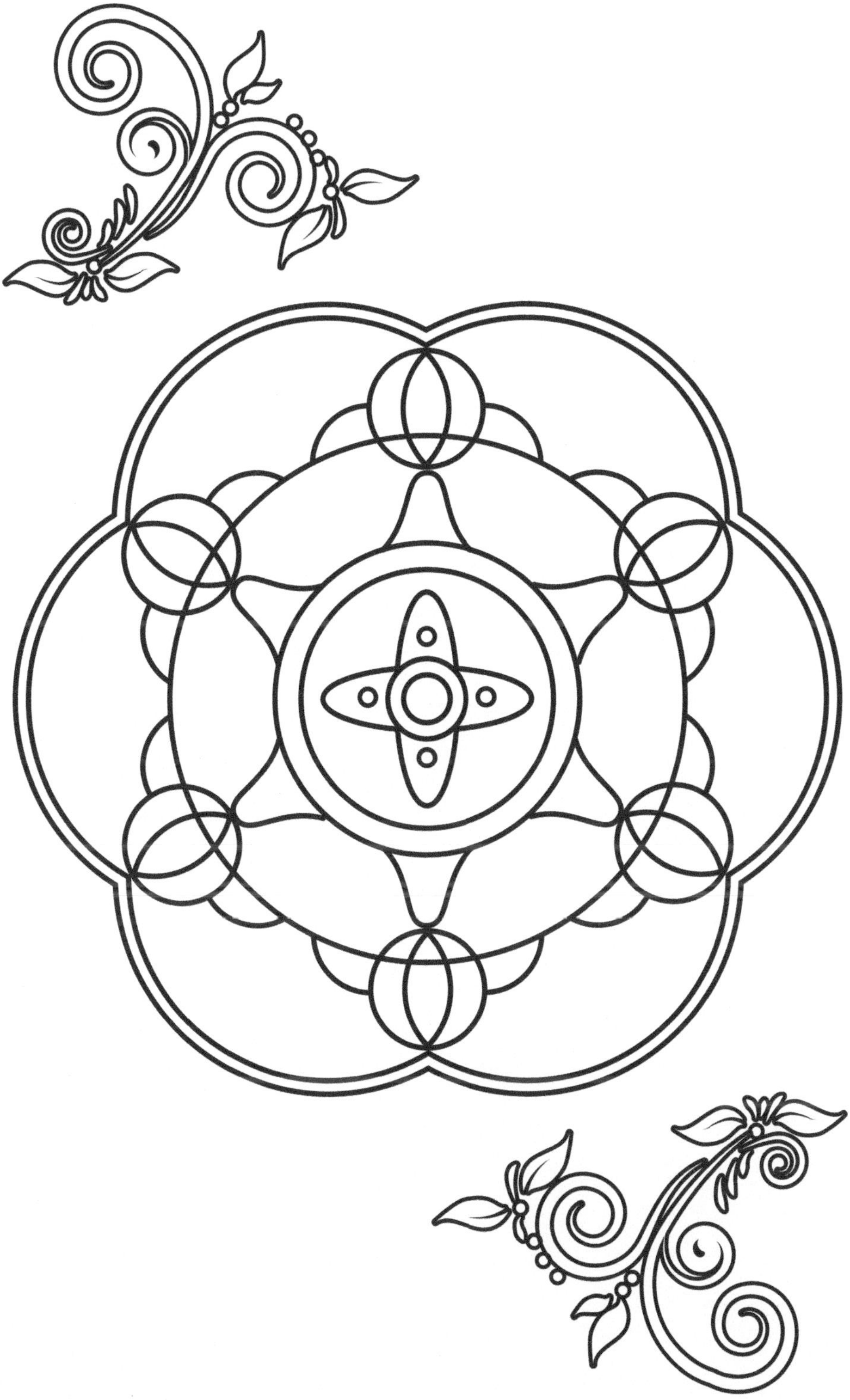

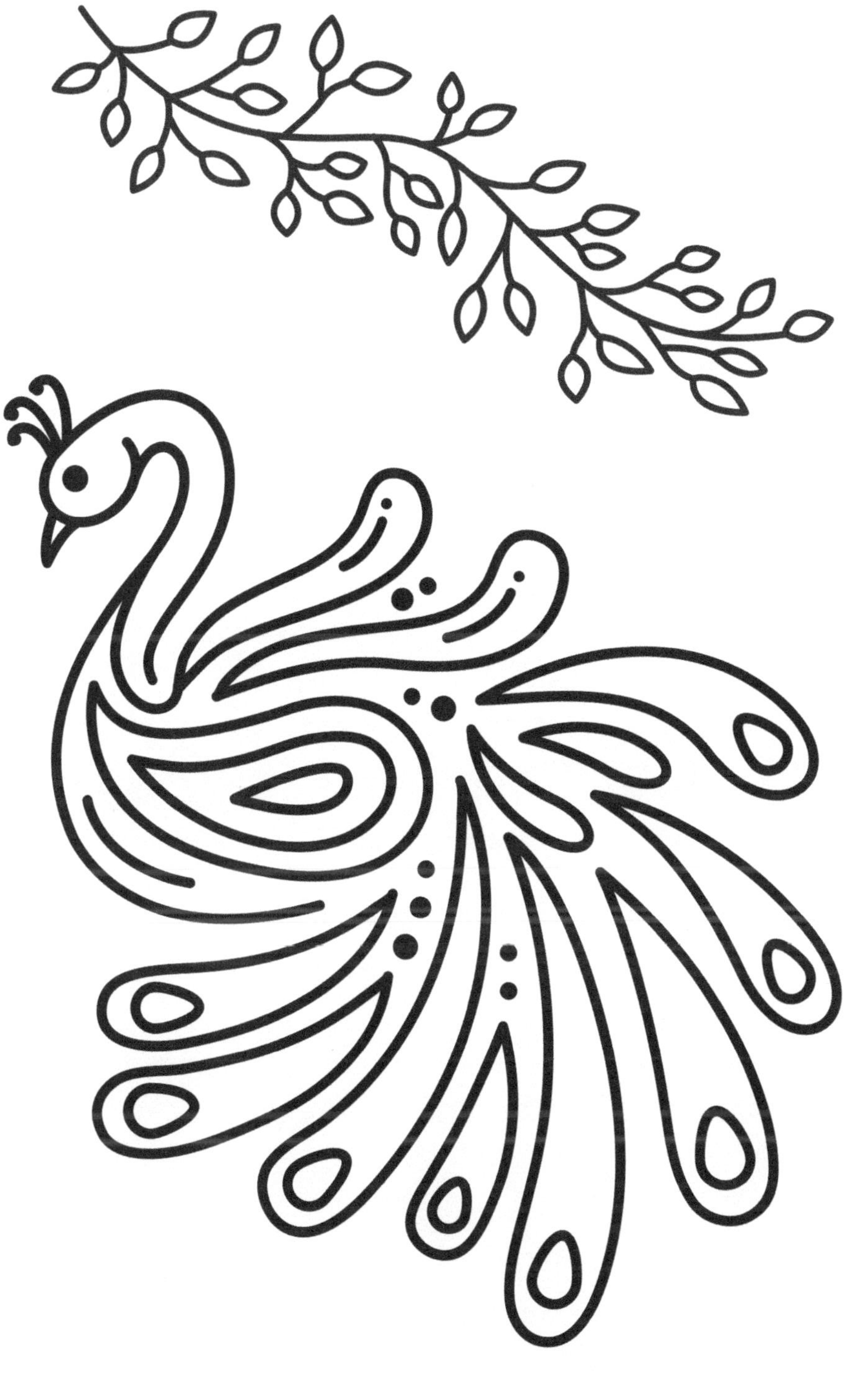

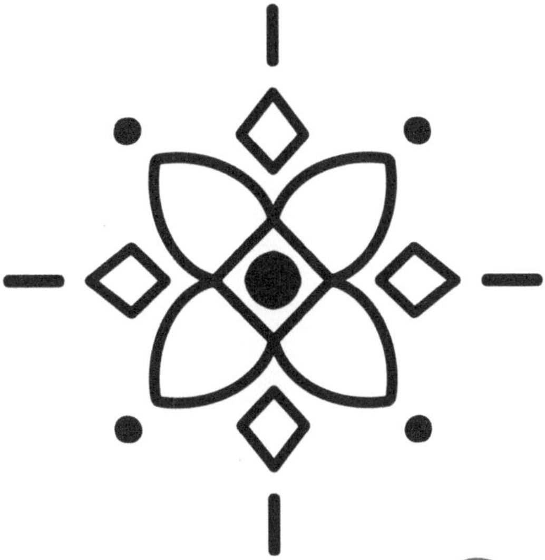

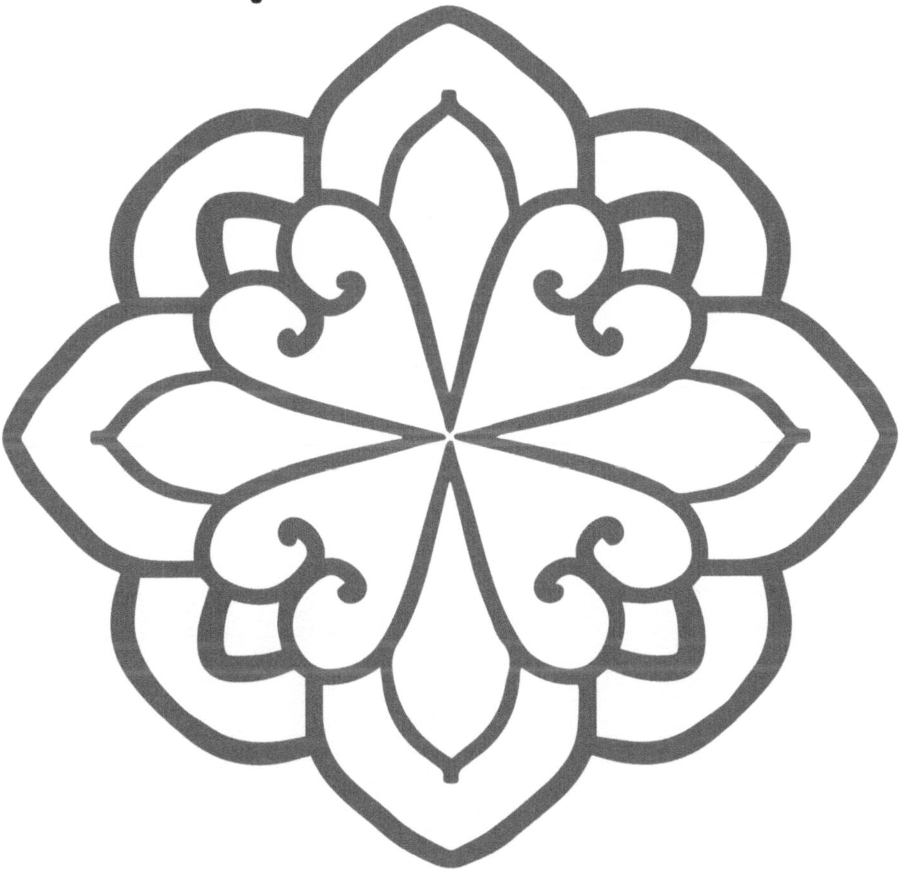

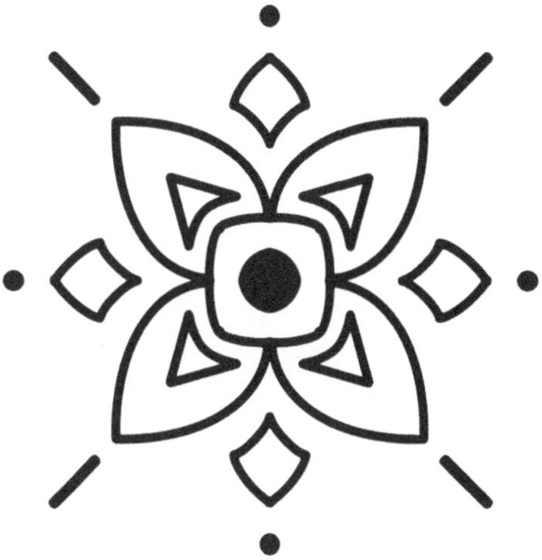

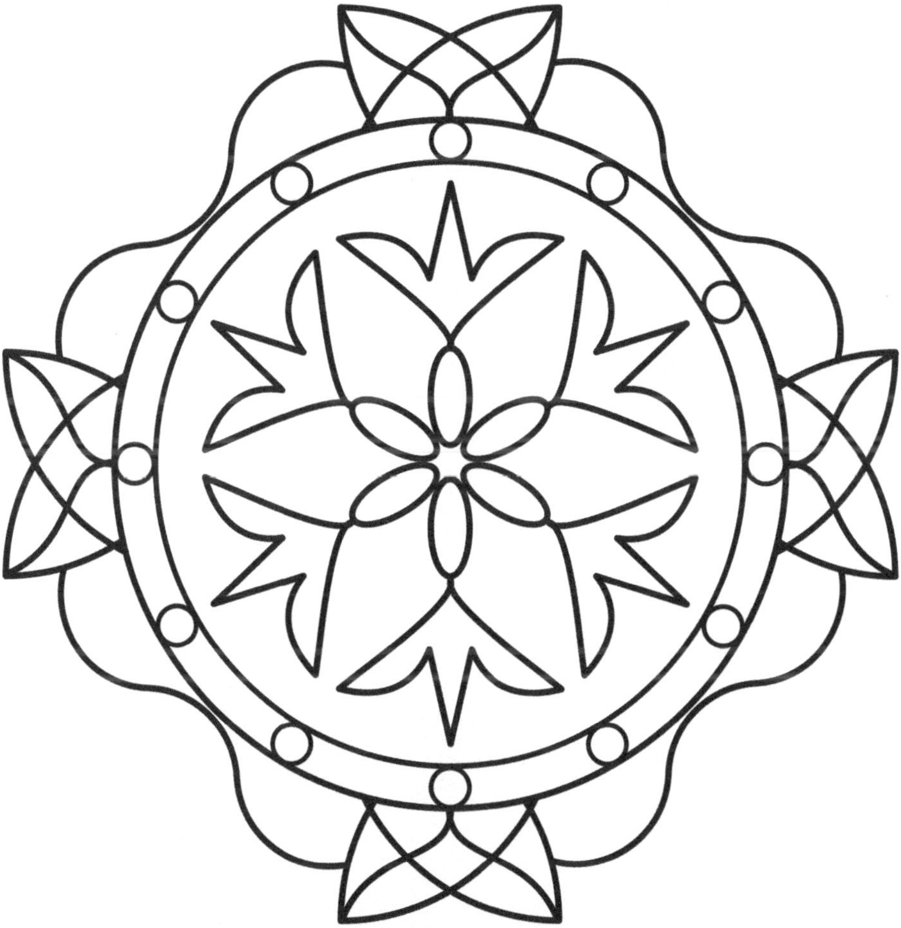

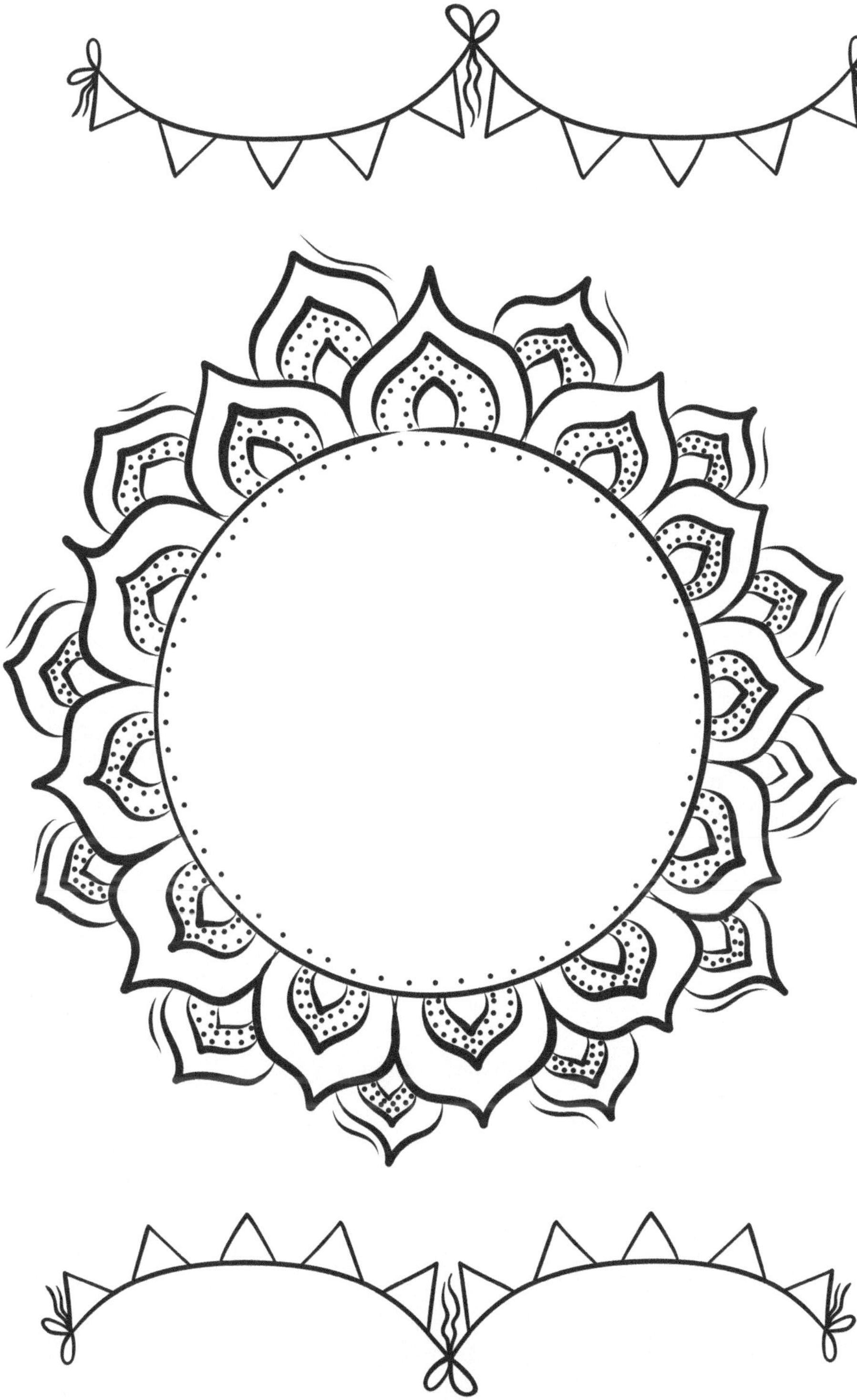

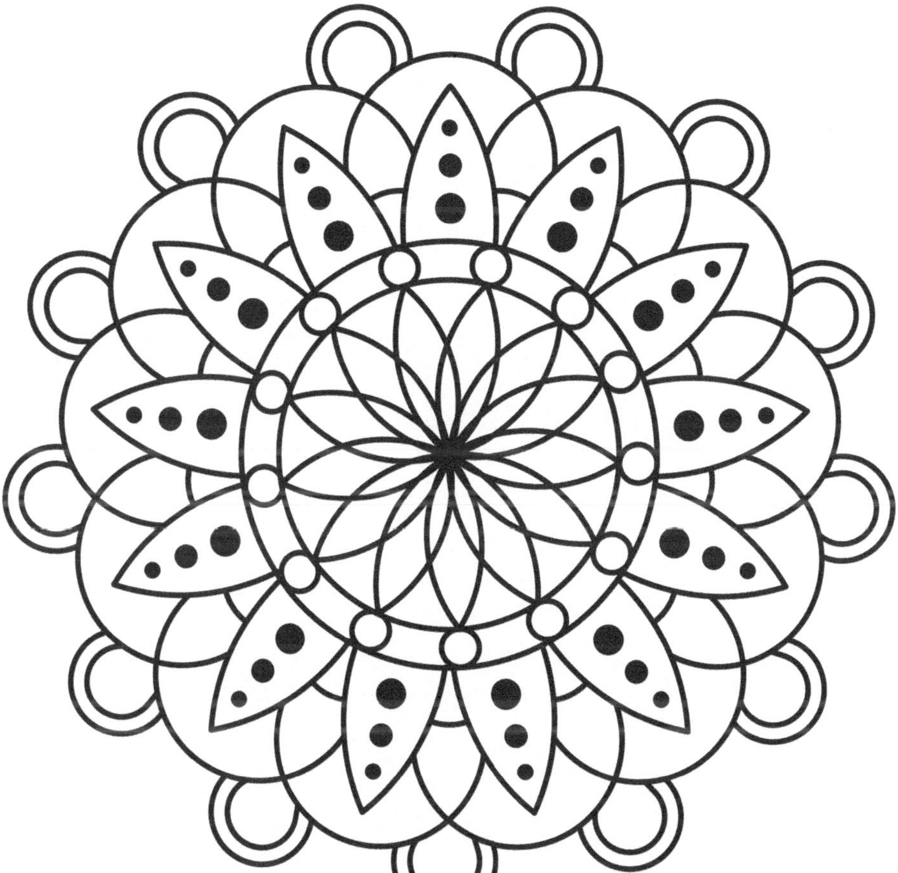

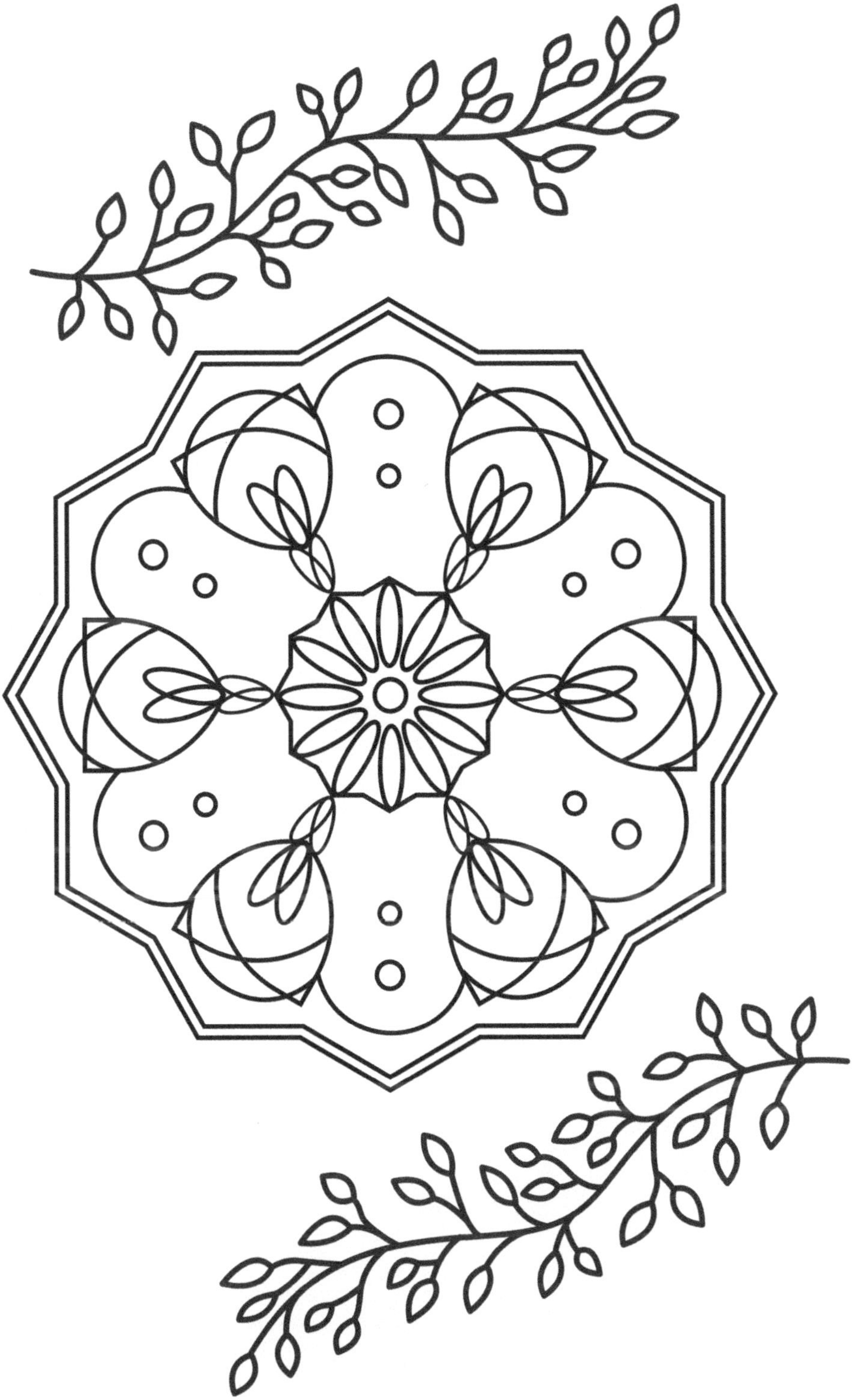

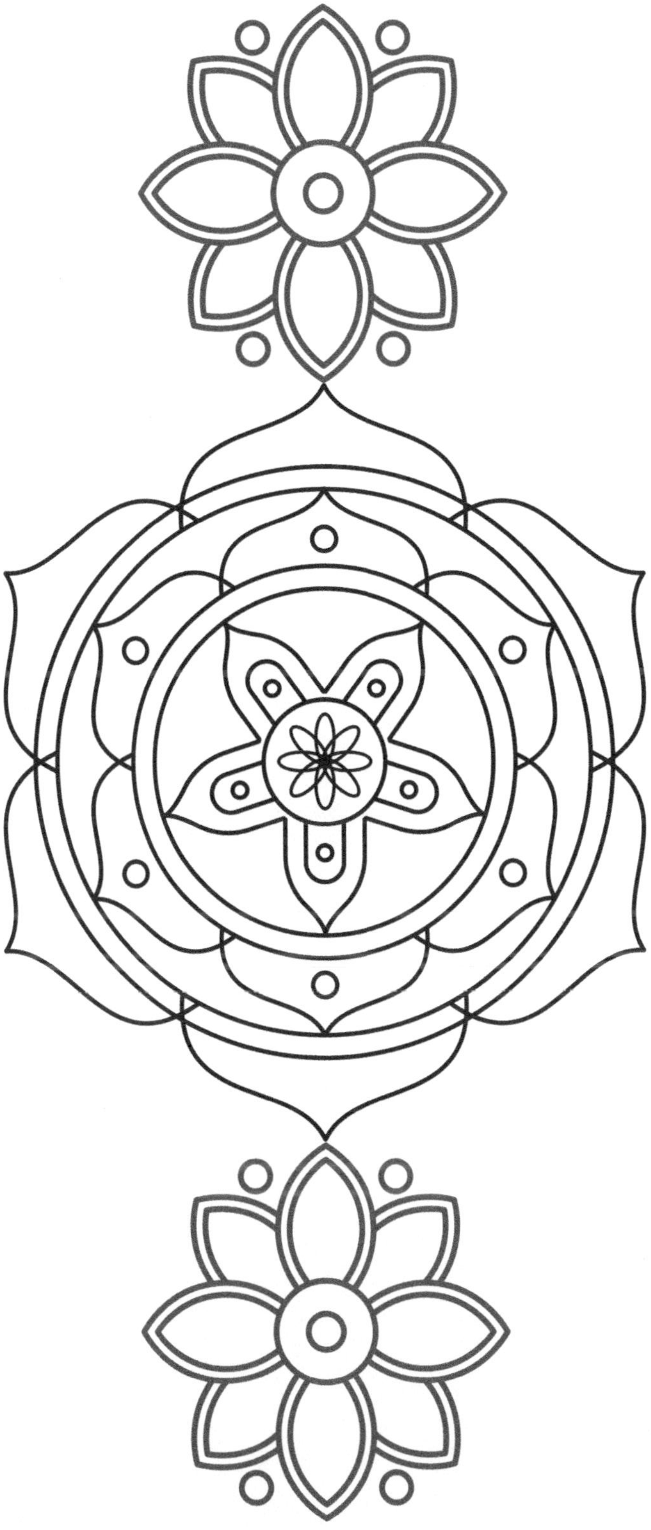

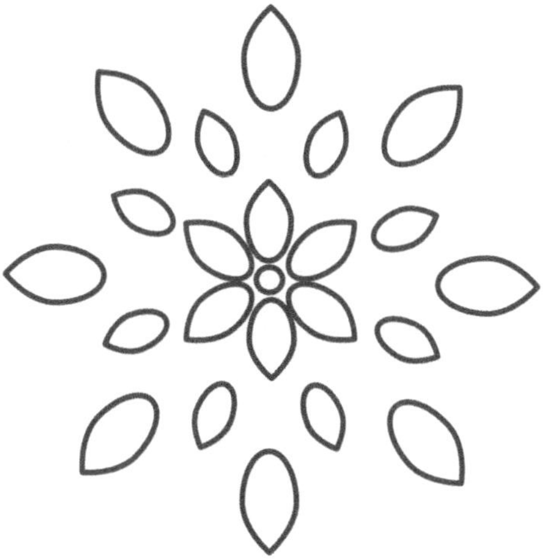
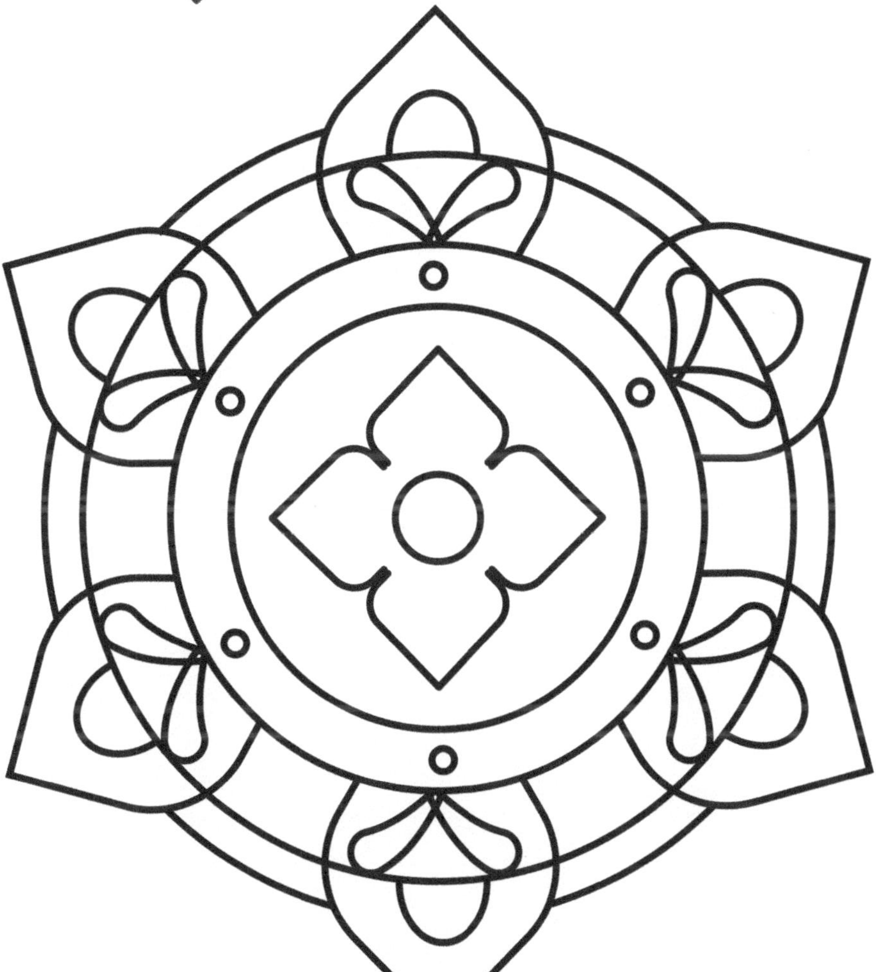

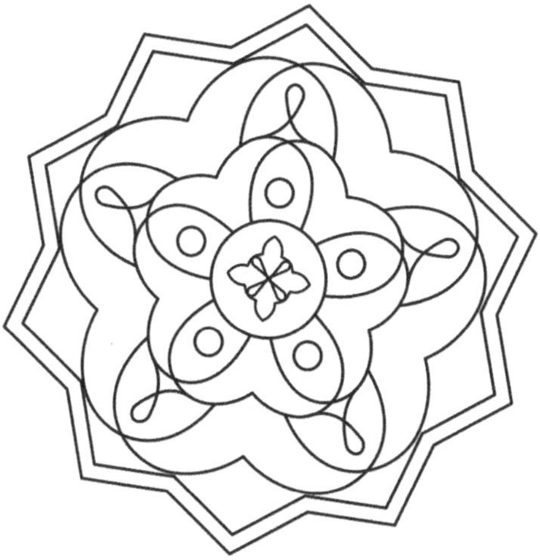

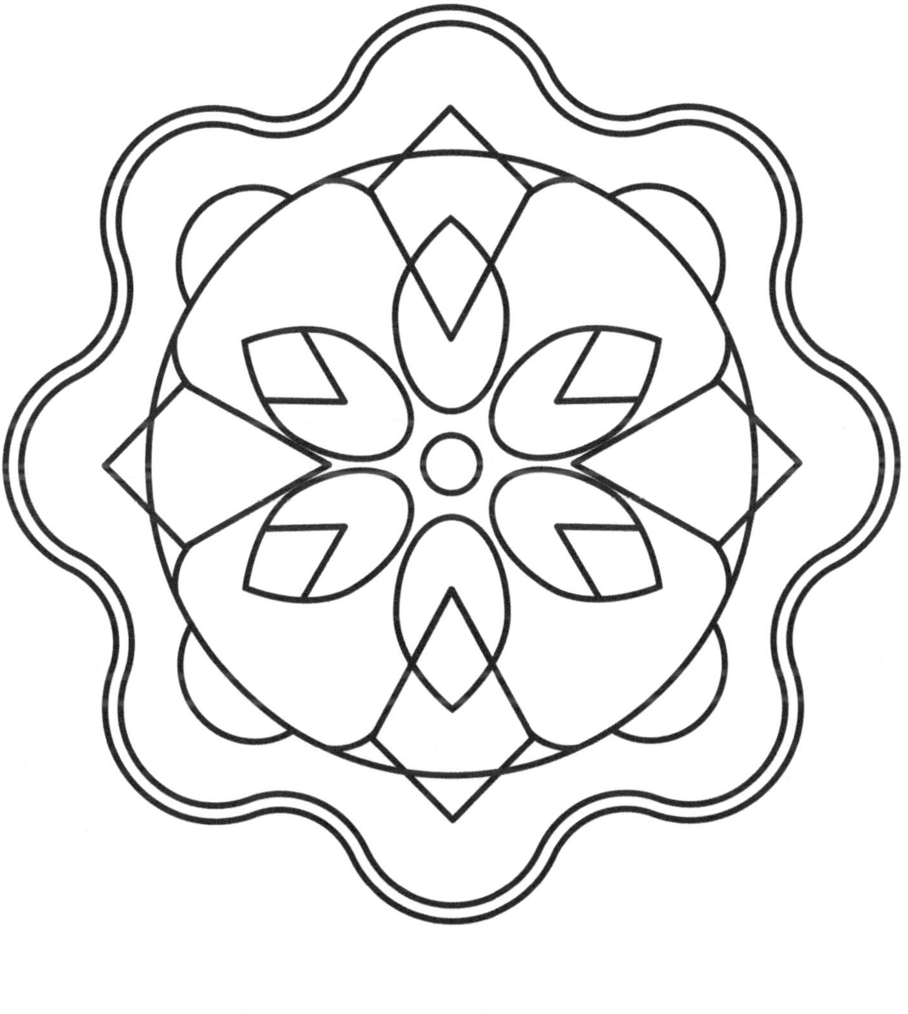

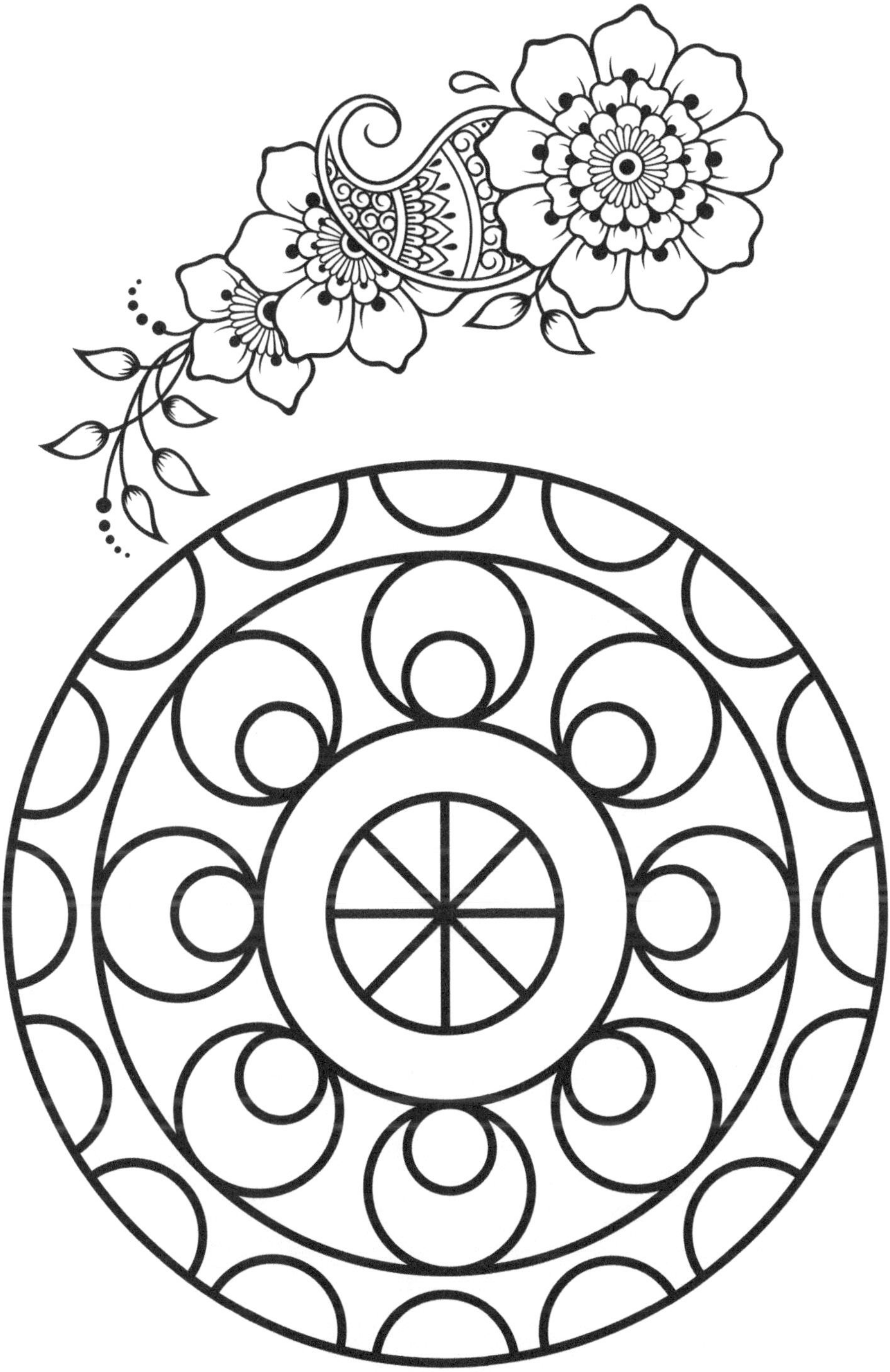

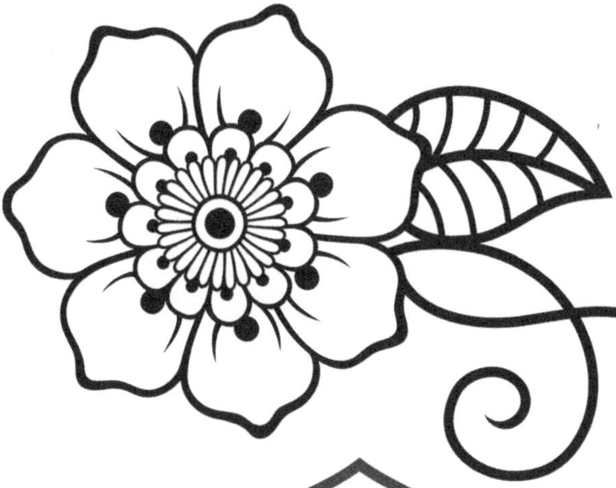

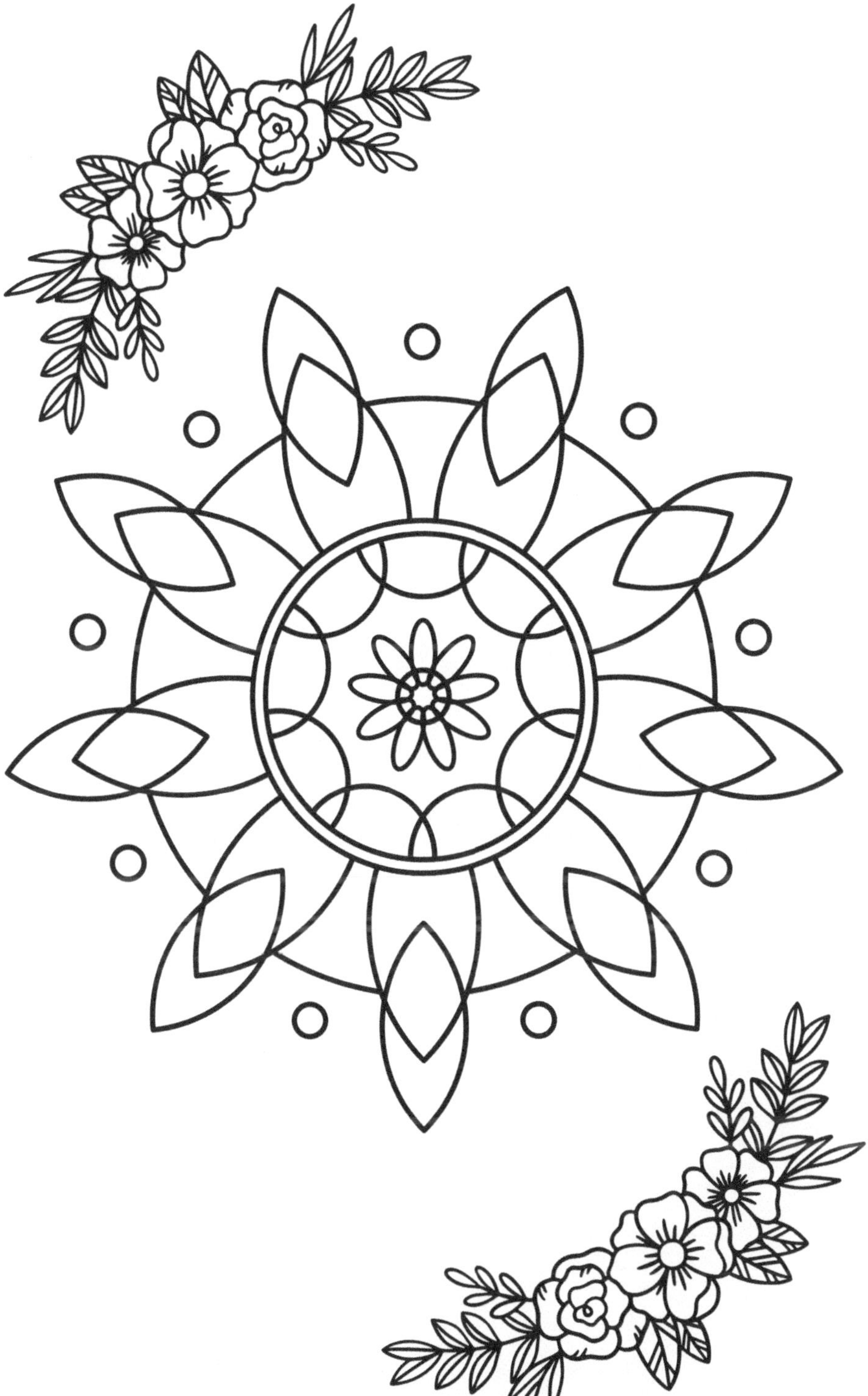

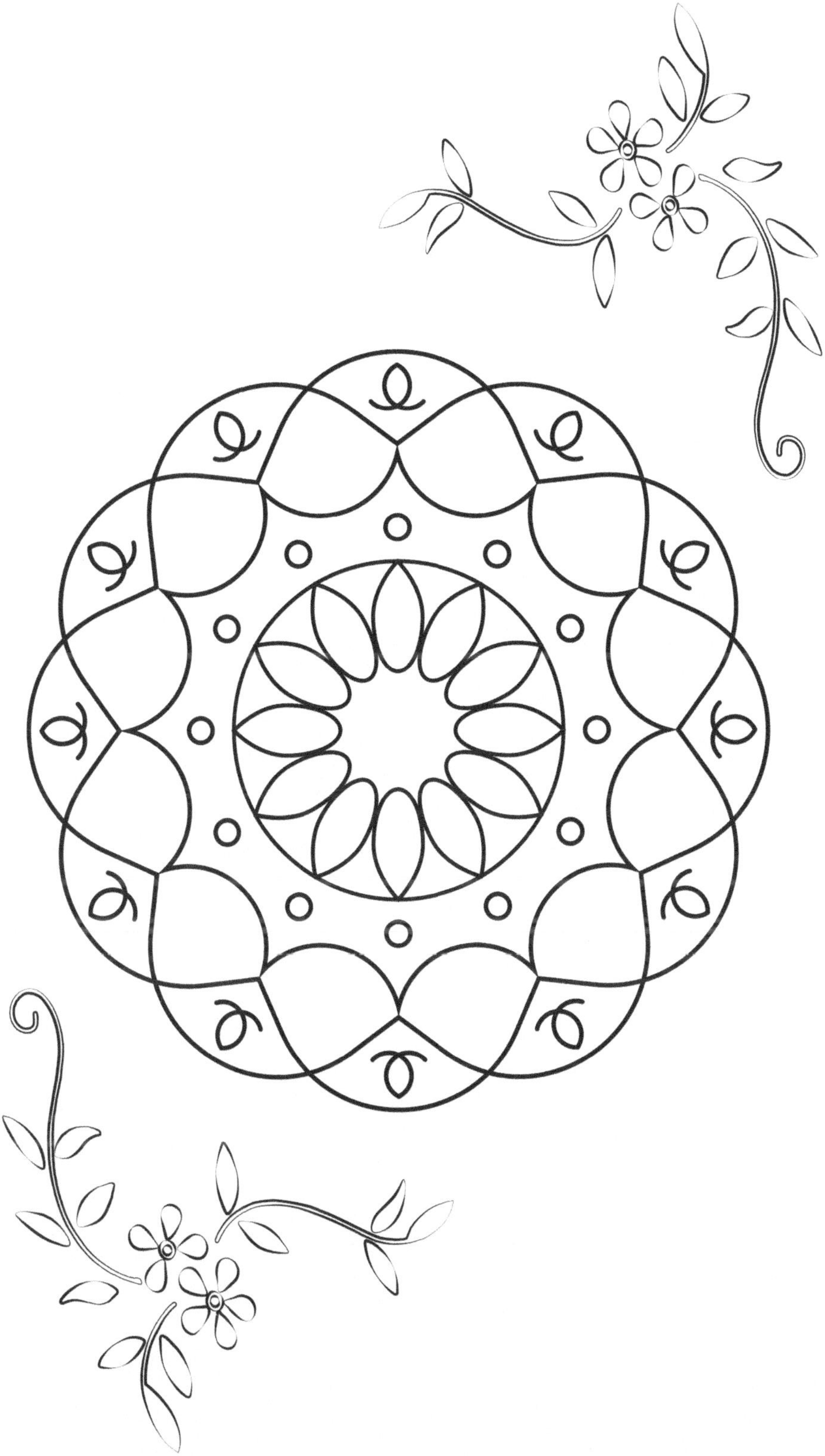

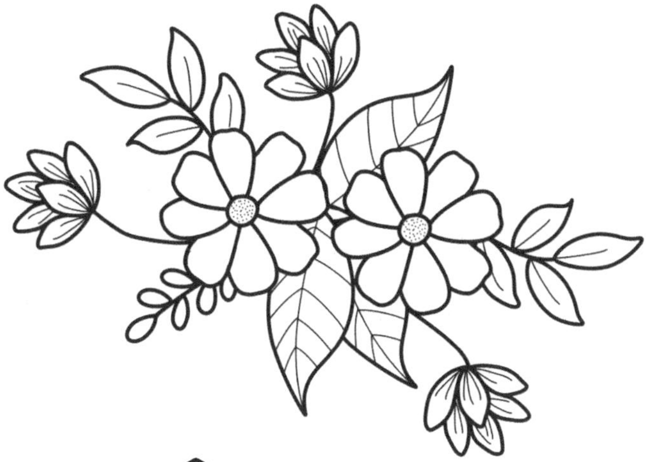

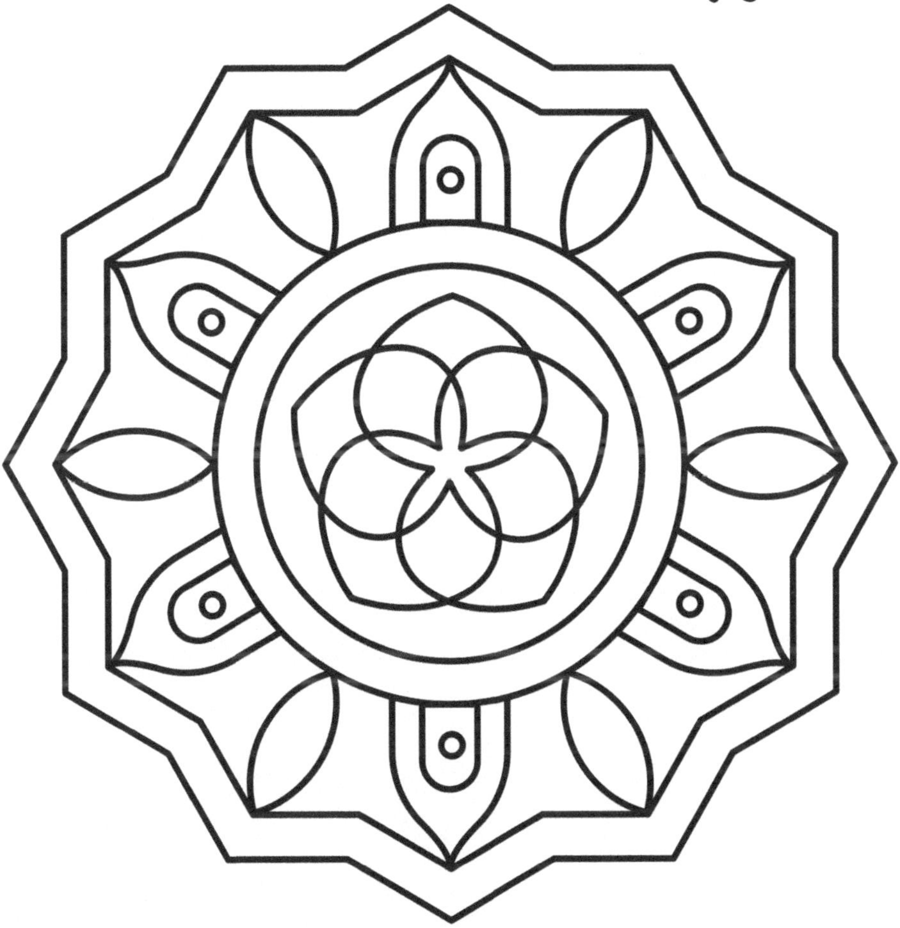

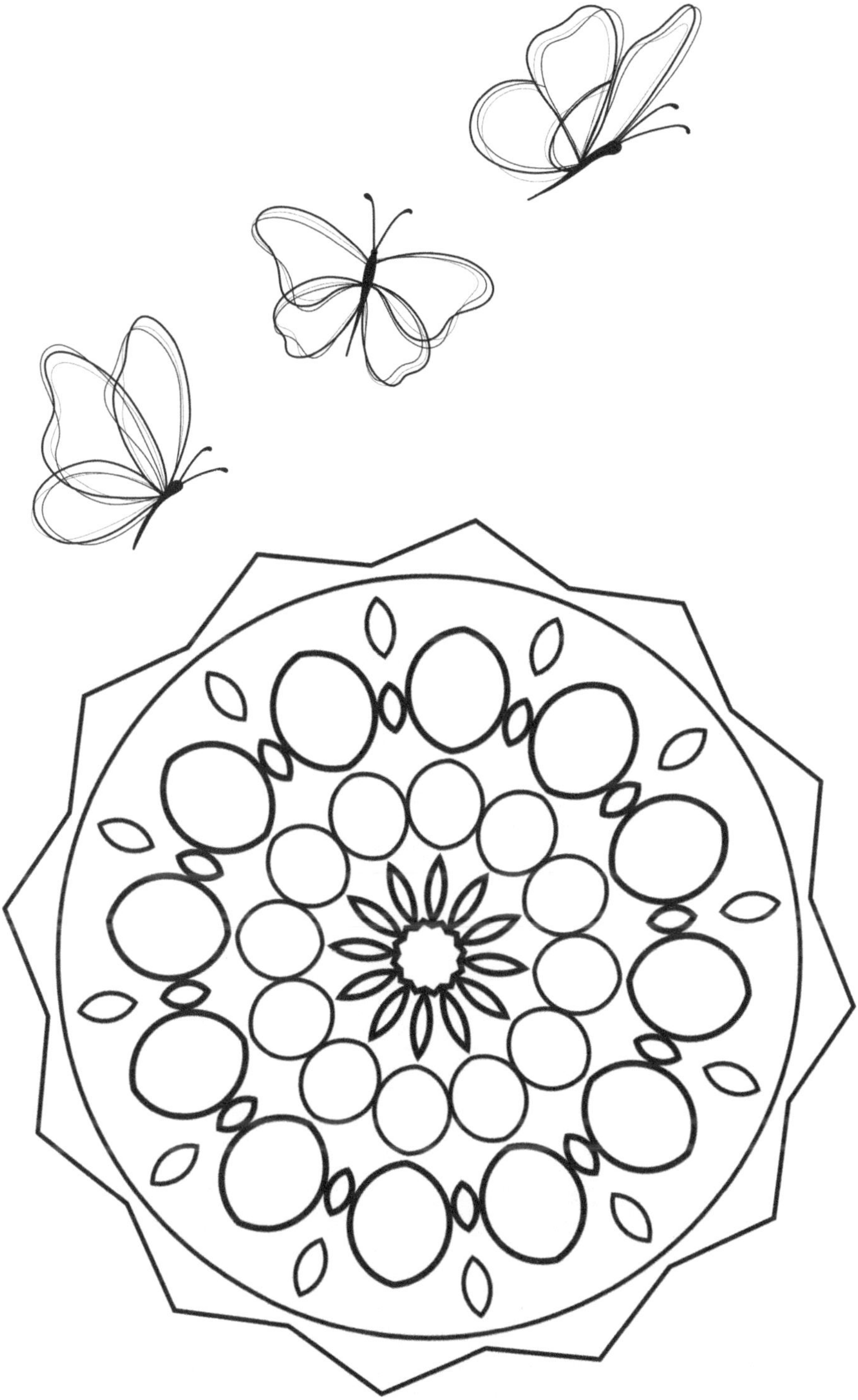

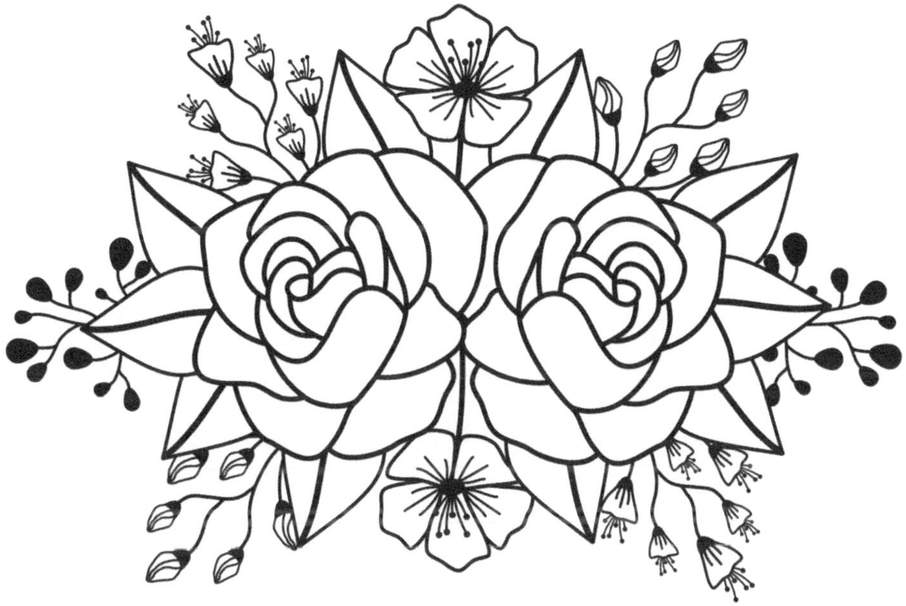

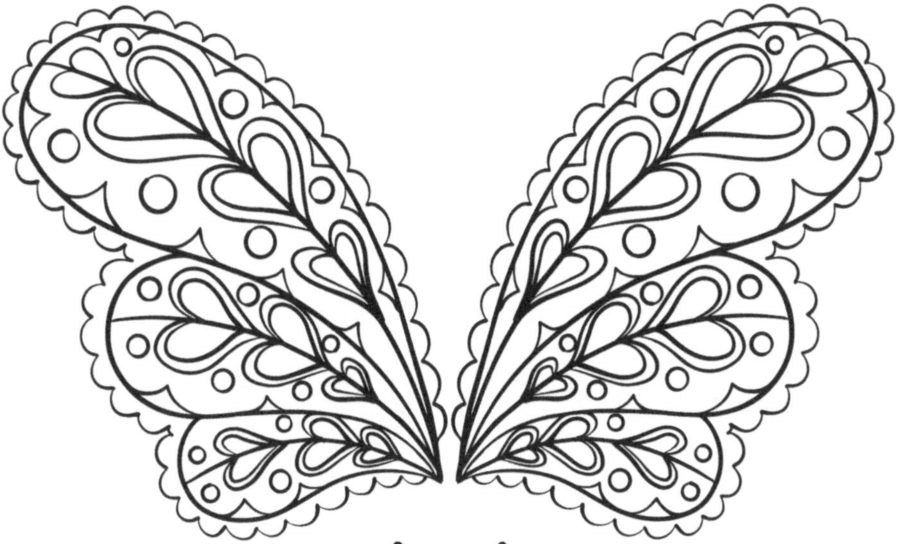

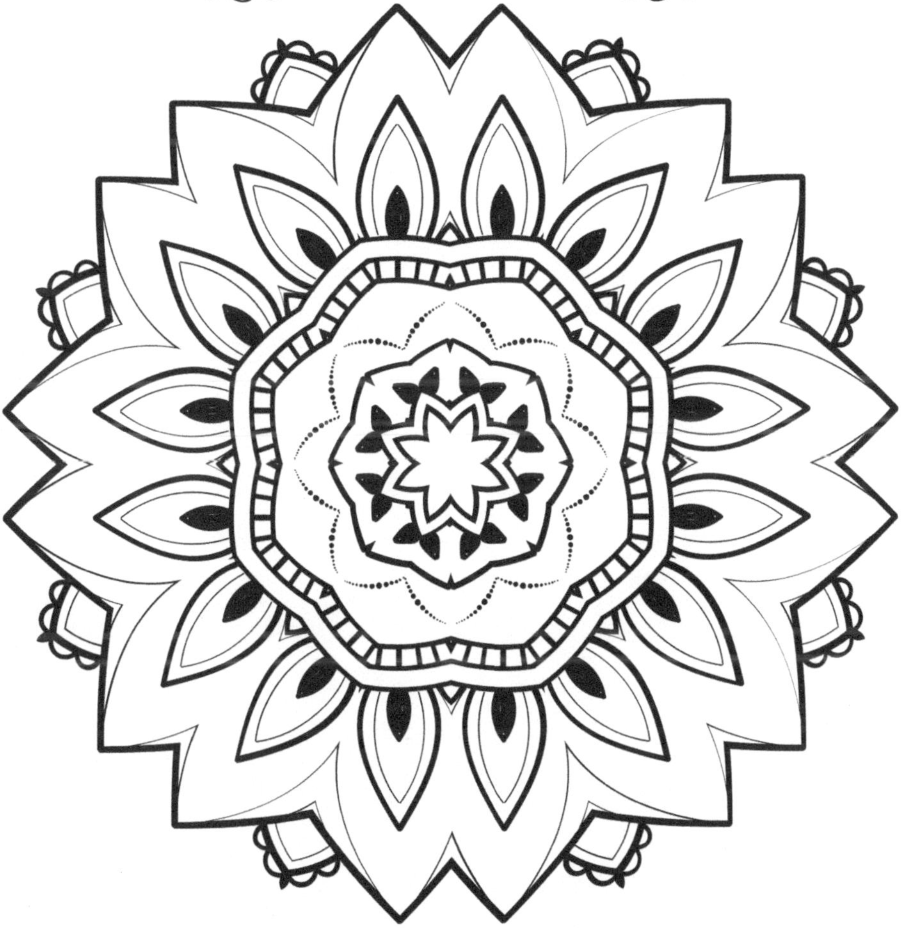

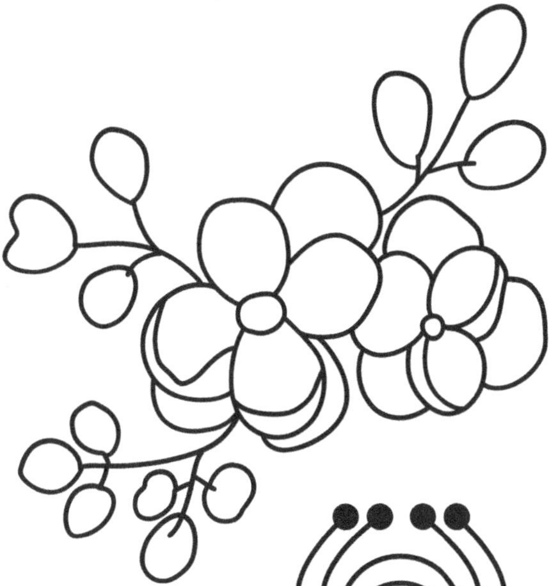

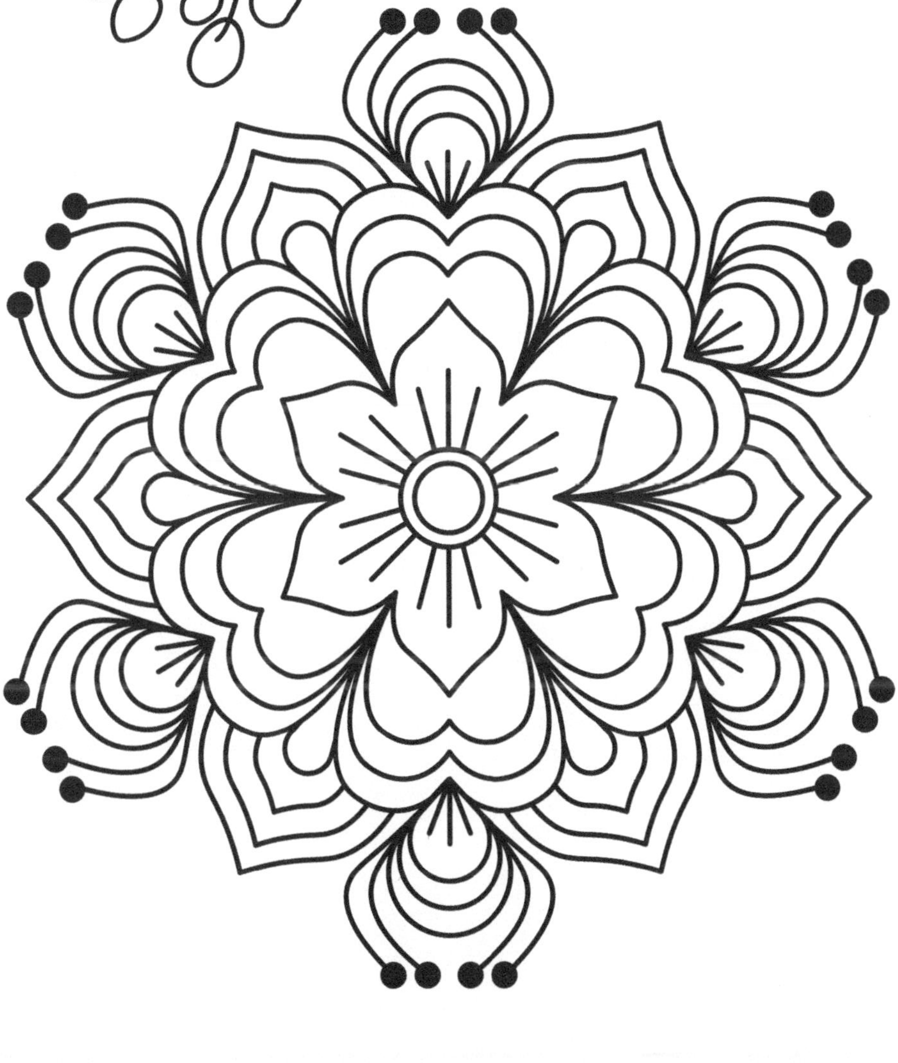

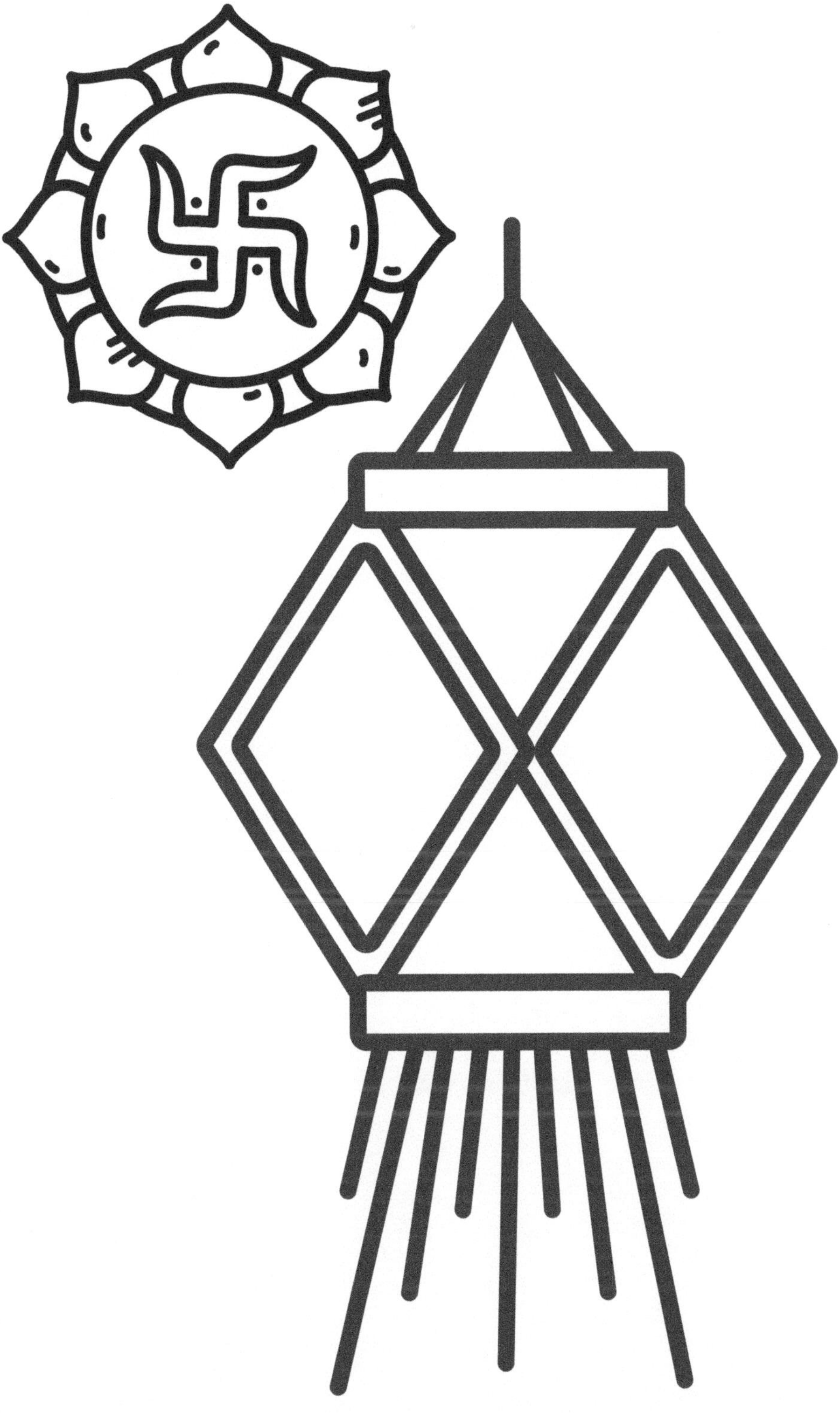

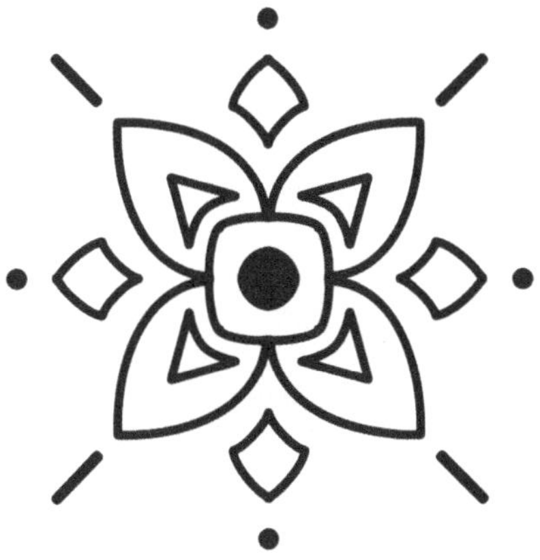
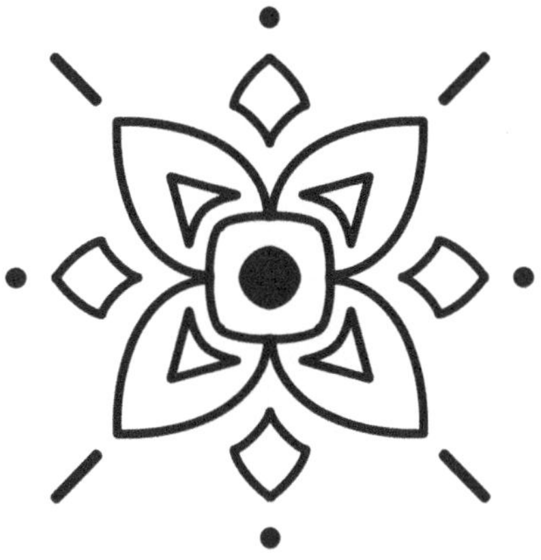
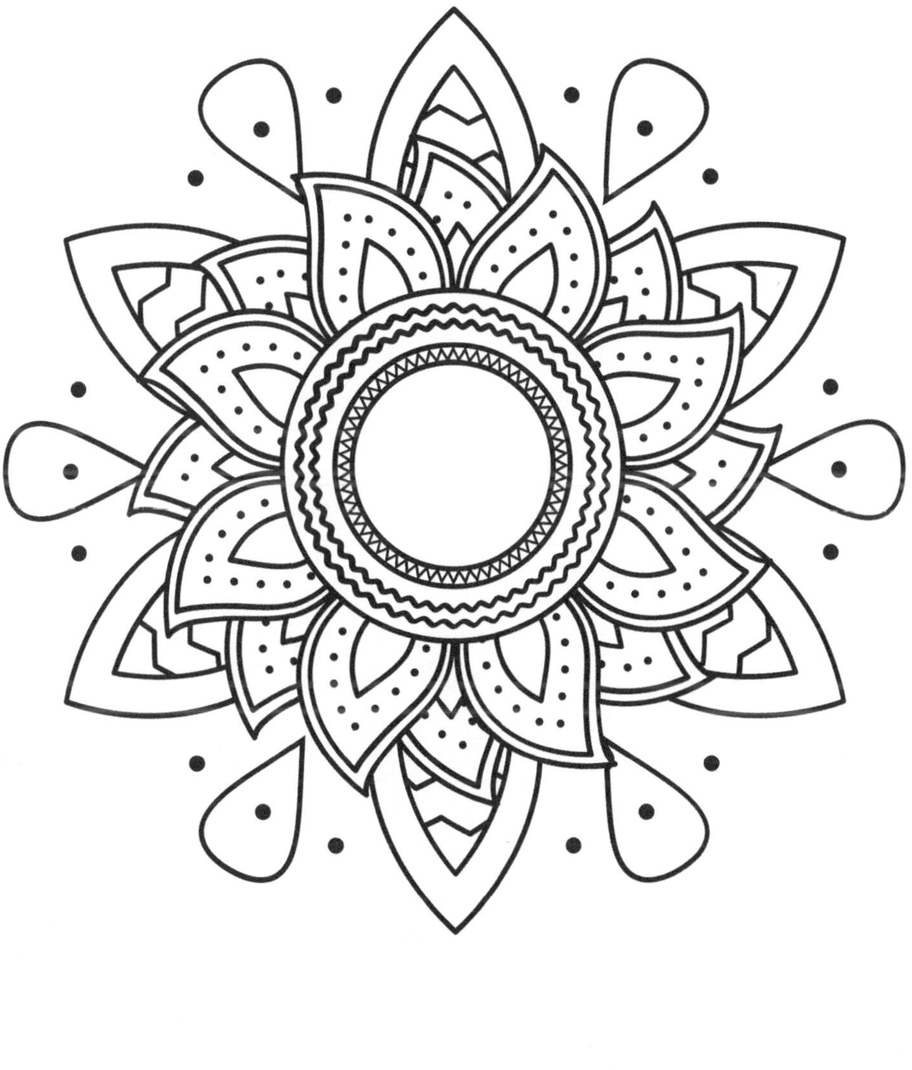

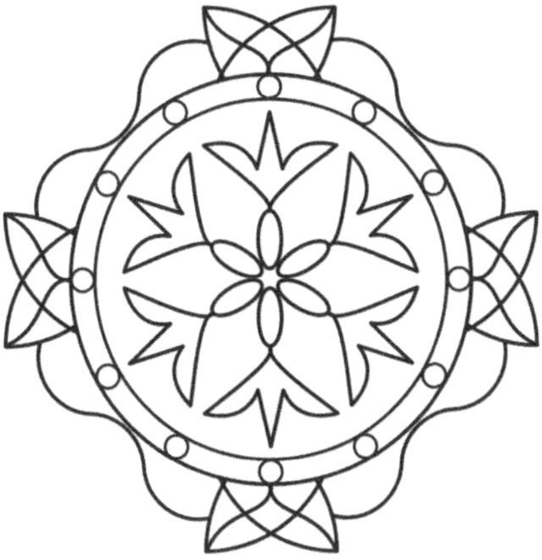

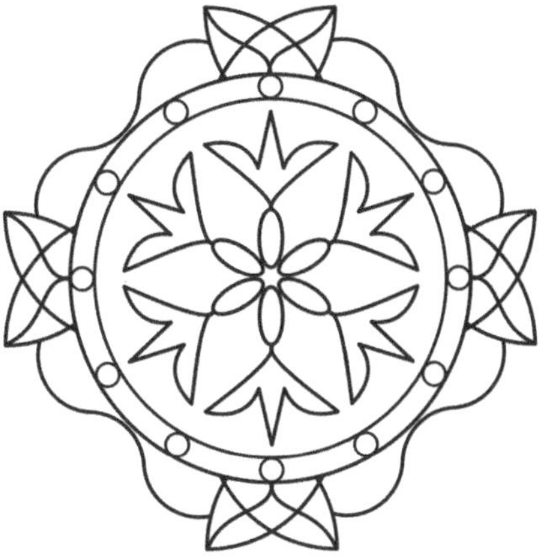

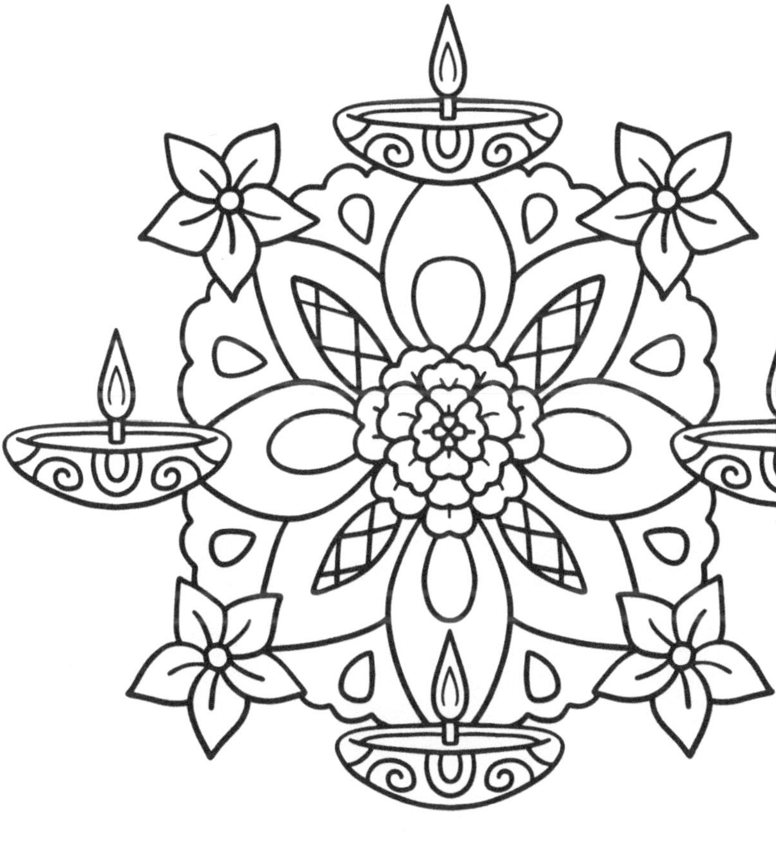

Made in United States
Cleveland, OH
25 October 2024

10309647R00046